THE MAKING OF
This Side of Paradise

JAMES L. W. WEST III

UNIVERSITY OF PENNSYLVANIA PRESS

PHILADELPHIA 1983

This work was published with the support of
the Haney Foundation.

Library of Congress Cataloging in Publication Data

West, James L. W. III
    The making of This side of Paradise.

    Includes index.
    1. Fitzgerald, F. Scott (Francis Scott), 1896–1940.
This side of paradise.   I. Title.
PS3511.I9T4839 1983   813'.52   82-21828
ISBN 0-8122-7867-4

In der Beschränkung
zeigt sich erst der Meister.
—Goethe

Contents

Acknowledgments

This book originated as my doctoral dissertation at the University of South Carolina in 1971. I revised the dissertation periodically over the next five years, and it was accepted for book publication by a small firm in Columbia, S.C., in the fall of 1976. Copies of that version were printed in the spring of 1977, but as they were being bound the publishing house failed. That early version was never advertised; no copies were distributed or sold. Bound books existed, but in the strict sense the study had not been published. The boxed and sealed books were stored in a Massachusetts warehouse until 1981, when I acquired the entire stock and had it destroyed. The present book represents a complete revision of the 1977 version.

My initial debt in this project is to Matthew J. Bruccoli, who directed my dissertation at South Carolina. I also thank Joseph Katz for many useful suggestions and for his support and interest. Alexander Clark, former curator of manuscripts at Princeton University Library, and his assistant, Mrs. Wanda Randall, were helpful in answering my queries and in giving me access to the Fitzgerald Papers. For financial support I thank the University of South Carolina for the 1970–71 Reynolds Fellowship, the Woodrow Wilson National Fellowship Foundation for a dissertation fellowship in 1971, and the National Humanities Center, where the final revision of this study was carried out in the fall of 1981. For other assistance I am grateful to Malcolm Call, Thomas L. McHaney, Anita Malebranche, Bryant Mangum, and Debby Stuart.

Introduction

> . . . to write it took three months;
> to conceive it—three minutes; to
> collect the data in it—all my life.
>
> —F. Scott Fitzgerald
> *The Author's Apology*

This book is a study of the gestation, composition, publication, reception, and textual history of F. Scott Fitzgerald's first novel, *This Side of Paradise*. The novel occupies an important place in Fitzgerald's career. Its lively reception and commercial success launched him as the "Prophet of the Jazz Age," the spokesman for his generation, and *This Side of Paradise* is one of the major reasons for his fame today. The novel is still read because it is at once dated and ageless. It was very much a product of its own times—the first (and still the most faithful) chronicle of American youth in transition from the nineteenth century into the twentieth. Fitzgerald recorded carefully the current fads of speech, behavior, dance, dress, and literature; and the novel is a period piece, in the best sense of that term. The novel is also an ageless revelation of the difficulties faced by a gifted aesthete who must grow and mature in a society which offers him no functional place. Amory Blaine, Fitzgerald's hero, searches throughout the novel for a proper stance toward the problems that face every talented young person: love, sex, religion, money, education, and art. The styles have changed; the essential problems are eternal. *This Side of Paradise* still speaks to young readers, who often discover it when the decisions that confront Amory first confront them; the novel also continues to remind older readers of what that youthful time was like. The composition of such an unusual work deserves careful study.

This Side of Paradise changed Fitzgerald's life and career. In a life that would see many successes, *This Side of Paradise* was his first big one—the first time he combined the magic ingredients of hard work, talent, and imagination to win the golden reward. The story of how he came to do that is fascinating in itself and is central to his eventual conception of his own early success and later disillusionment. This study covers the initial few years in his professional career and reveals how he fashioned his first full-length work of literature. The narrative recreates his working methods and compositional habits: with *This Side of Paradise* Fitzgerald developed techniques that he would refine and perfect during the later years of his career.

A significant part of the story deals with commercial book production in the 1920s, an important period that saw publication of the first efforts of William Faulkner, Thomas Wolfe, and Ernest Hemingway. Hemingway and Wolfe were published by Charles Scribner's Sons, and both were under the wing of Scribner's most famous editor, Maxwell Perkins. When *This Side of Paradise* went to Scribner's, Perkins was a young editor there. In part through his work on this novel, he learned to discover, develop, and edit the authors who today occupy significant positions in the literature of America's twenties and thirties. This book is therefore a chapter in the story of Maxwell Perkins.[1]

1. An excellent recent biography of Perkins is A. Scott Berg, *Max Perkins: Editor of Genius* (New York: Dutton, 1978).

"Story" is the word I have chosen to use so far, because that is what I have tried to make this book do: tell the important and little-known story of how a famous writer came to start his career. But this book is essentially a serious work of textual scholarship. It is an investigation into the strange history of *This Side of Paradise*, designed to show readers of the novel how far distant they are from what Fitzgerald originally wrote and wanted to publish. The text of this novel is notoriously bad, a fact noted by reviewers when it first appeared and commented upon by critics ever since. There are worse texts in American literature (prepublication cutting and tampering marred *Look Homeward, Angel* and *Absalom, Absalom!* and postpublication corruption damaged *The Wild Palms* and *The Great Gatsby*, for example), but for careless error *This Side of Paradise* probably has no contemporary equal. Fitzgerald's spelling was bad, and his grammar and punctuation were idiosyncratic to say the least. As a result *This Side of Paradise* is marred by numerous sins against the mechanics of the English language. It is also an immature and derivative novel, filled with half-formed ideas and transparent poses. *This Side of Paradise* is open to criticism, but one must not confuse its mechanical and grammatical failings with its literary merit. Unfortunately the condition of its text has caused many readers to do just that. As published in 1920, the novel caused Fitzgerald to be branded a muddleheaded pseudo-intellectual, a tag that is still sometimes applied to him.

These several concerns cannot be separated one from another, and I have not tried to do so. Instead I have presented a blend of textual, biographical, and critical scholarship, with the textual approach foremost. My method has been to sketch in the important details of Fitzgerald's life for the years during which he wrote *This Side of Paradise* and to examine, with care and precision, the documents that survive from the making of the novel. As occasions have arisen I have discussed points of critical interpretation, especially when new evidence from the manuscripts has a significant effect on how one should read a passage. I have not attempted, however, to provide a full critical interpretation of the novel. Other scholars have already done so: *This Side of Paradise* has probably attracted as much critical commentary as it deserves, and there are no great mysteries about its meaning.[2] There are, however, intriguing questions about its composition and textual history. These I have concentrated on.

The surviving fragments of *The Romantic Egotist* and the

2. The best article-length study is Clinton S. Burhans, Jr., "Structure and Theme in *This Side of Paradise*," *JEGP* 68 (1969):605–24. Also worth consulting are Sy Kahn, "*This Side of Paradise:* The Pageantry of Disillusion," *Midwest Quarterly* 7 (1966): 177–94; and James W. Tuttleton, "The Presence of Poe in *This Side of Paradise*," *English Language Notes* 3 (1966):284–89. Arthur Mizener's criticisms in his *The Far Side of Paradise*, rev. ed. (Boston: Houghton Mifflin, 1965), pp. 90–98, are worthwhile, as are the comments by Robert Sklar in *F. Scott Fitzgerald: The Last Laocoön* (New York: Oxford University Press, 1967), pp. 25–57. Sklar is particularly good on the critical reception of *This Side of Paradise* (see p. 109 ff). Intelligent discussions may be found in James E. Miller, *F. Scott Fitzgerald: His Art and His Technique* (New York: New York University Press, 1964), pp. 1–44; and in Kenneth Eble, *F. Scott Fitzgerald* (New York: Twayne Publishers, 1963), pp. 42–51. Although marred by factual errors, Milton R. Stern's comments in *The Golden Moment: The Novels of F. Scott Fitzgerald* (Urbana: University of Illinois Press, 1971), pp. 3–106, are illuminating, especially his comparison of *This Side of Paradise* with Compton Mackenzie's *Sinister Street*. Also provocative, and also marred by factual errors, is Madelyn Hoffmann, "*This Side of Paradise:* A Study in Pathological Narcissism," *Literature and Psychology* 28 (1978): 178–85. A limited but useful attempt to examine and discuss the fragments of *The Romantic Egotist* and the manuscript of *This Side of Paradise* is found in Henry Dan Piper, *F. Scott Fitzgerald: A Critical Portrait* (New York: Holt, 1965), pp. 37–63. An excellent recent article which identifies many of the contemporary references in the novel is Lynn Haywood, "Historical Notes for *This Side of Paradise*," *Resources for American Literary Study* 10 (1980): 191–208. A more limited and less successful attempt to do the same kind of thing is Dorothy Ballweg Good, "'A Romance and a Reading List': The Literary References in *This Side of Paradise*," *Fitzgerald/Hemingway Annual 1976*, pp. 35–64.

manuscript of *This Side of Paradise* are on restriction to me, and I have been unable to quote directly from them. Fortunately, however, nearly all of the passages one needs for a study of this kind have appeared in print already, in one form or another, in the great mass of Fitzgerald scholarship published over the past three decades. I have therefore quoted from published texts and have had to use paraphrase or description in only a very few instances.

Fitzgerald was inaccurate (and sometimes inspired) in his spelling and punctuating. Most of the published texts from which I quote in this study fortunately preserve his mistakes in orthography and pointing. I have retained these errors whenever the text I am quoting reproduces them. Some editors, however, have corrected Fitzgerald's mistakes; in these instances (Turnbull's edition of letters, for example) I have quoted the published texts in order to comply with the restrictions of the Fitzgerald estate.

This book is not intended exclusively for Fitzgerald specialists, nor is it aimed solely at textual scholars. Rather, it is written for persons interested in Fitzgerald's writings and career, and in the times in which he lived and wrote. The only preparation one needs for this study is a fresh reading of *This Side of Paradise*. I have avoided textual jargon, and I have kept footnoting to a minimum—without, I trust, sacrificing exactness of documentation or proper scholarly decorum. The resulting narrative should increase the reader's understanding of F. Scott Fitzgerald's first novel—of how he wrote it and of what he wanted it to say.

September 1982   JAMES L. W. WEST III

THE MAKING OF
This Side of Paradise

1

Beginnings

November 1917–July 1919

Beside the date November 1917 in his personal ledger F. Scott Fitzgerald wrote the words "Begun novel."[1] This date marks the point at which he began to put together the novel that would be published on 26 March 1920 as *This Side of Paradise*. Although this was Fitzgerald's first book-length effort, he was by no means an inexperienced author. In fact much material from his apprentice writings would eventually be incorporated into his novel. Fitzgerald was twenty-one years old, and for eight of those years he had been publishing creative work—poetry, fiction, humor, lyrics, and drama. When he embarked on his first novel, he had already served a lengthy amateur apprenticeship.

Throughout his school years at St. Paul Academy (1908–11), at Newman School in Hackensack, New Jersey (1911–13), and at Princeton University (1913–17), Fitzgerald had devoted much time and energy to writing. By November 1917 he had published in school literary journals and newspapers some thirteen short stories, two one-act plays, five book reviews, and six poems; and he had written four plays for the Elizabethan Dramatic Club in his native St. Paul. He had con-

1. *F. Scott Fitzgerald's Ledger: A Facsimile* (Washington, D.C.: Microcard Editions, 1972), p. 172.

tributed to Princeton's *Nassau Literary Magazine* and to the *Princeton Tiger*, and he had written lyrics for three musical comedies performed by the Princeton Triangle Club. For one so young, Fitzgerald's writing experience was unusually varied and his total production extensive.

But writing a novel for commercial publication and sale is quite different from turning out stories for school publications or lyrics for college musicals. In November 1917 Fitzgerald was still a talented amateur who had much to learn about professional authorship. Talent, he would come to realize, was not enough. The composition of *This Side of Paradise* taught him that lesson, and the account of the making of the novel is a story of his growing professionalism. He learned how to organize and present his material and how to discipline his imagination without stifling it. He also learned for the first time how to salvage and reuse old material. But Fitzgerald learned by doing, learned as he wrote, and the published novel shows evidence of his trial-and-error method. Indeed, the story of *This Side of Paradise* is not entirely positive. Some of Fitzgerald's work was hasty and amateurish. In his hurry he was careless and took cut-and-paste shortcuts that in the end damaged the published novel.

One understands the strengths and weaknesses of *This Side of Paradise* better when one knows the circumstances behind its creation. A detailed account of the composition of the novel does not make it a better work of art, but it does reveal important information about the structuring of the book, about its narrative tone and point-of-view, and about the depiction of its central character, Amory Blaine.

Fitzgerald began serious work on his book in November 1917, but his actual decision to write a novel came earlier. It is difficult, however, to date that decision precisely. Fitzgerald had considered a book-length performance in some genre as early as the spring of 1917, but his initial impulse was to write a book of verse. In 1920 he recalled:

> I had decided that poetry was the only thing worth while, so with my head ringing with the meters of Swinburne and the matters of Rupert Brooke I spent the spring doing sonnets, ballads and rondels into the small hours. I had read somewhere that every great poet had written great poetry before he was twenty-one. I had only a year and, besides, war was impending. I must publish a book of startling verse before I was engulfed.[2]

But by the fall of 1917 Fitzgerald had discarded the idea of a book of poetry in favor of a novel that would combine both prose and verse. The novel was to be *The Romantic Egotist*, substantial parts of which he eventually revised and incorporated into *This Side of Paradise*.

To look ahead briefly: *The Romantic Egotist* was written from October 1917 to March 1918, submitted to Charles Scribner's Sons in May 1918, turned down for the first time in mid-August 1918, revised by Fitzgerald and submitted again in September 1918, and again rejected by Scribner's in October 1918. This rejected manuscript formed the basis for *This Side of Paradise*, which was assembled by Fitzgerald during the summer of 1919 and accepted by Scribner's in September of that year.

In October 1917 Fitzgerald was at Princeton waiting for approval of his Army officer's commission. The United States had entered World War I, and many of Fitzgerald's friends were al-

---

2. "Who's Who—and Why," *Saturday Evening Post*, 18 Sept. 1920, p. 61; repr. *Afternoon of an Author*, ed Arthur Mizener (Princeton: Princeton University Library, 1957), pp. 83–86.

ready in the military. He had decided not to continue his desultory college career; he was passing time by reading, helping his friend John Biggs edit the *Nassau Lit*, and attending lectures in English and philosophy. During the fall he made a start on *The Romantic Egotist*. In late October his commission came through, and he prepared to leave for training camp at Fort Leavenworth, Kansas. He had several chapters completed, and before he left he showed them to Christian Gauss, a member of the Princeton faculty. Gauss, later dean of Princeton, was one of Fitzgerald's mentors in college and eventually became his friend and occasional correspondent. Years later Gauss remembered that the first part of Fitzgerald's manuscript resembled the eventual opening of *This Side of Paradise*. The rest, however, was a mish-mash of "unconnected anecdotes, satires, and verse about Princeton life."[3] Fitzgerald urged Gauss to recommend the manuscript (once it was completed) to Charles Scribner's Sons, his own publisher, but Gauss would not do so, despite Fitzgerald's insistence that he would probably be killed in the war.

Fitzgerald was undaunted by this early setback and returned to his novel as soon as he was settled in Army camp. He had set his mind firmly on placing it with Scribner's, a conservative and prestigious house that handled such authors as James M. Barrie, George Meredith, John Galsworthy, Henry James, Edith Wharton, and Robert Louis Stevenson. Fitzgerald had another contact with Scribner's besides Gauss, and he began to use it. Through Monsignor Sigourney Fay, a priest whom he had known at Newman School and to whom *This Side of Paradise* was eventually dedicated, Fitzgerald had met and talked with Shane Leslie, an Irish Catholic writer whose American publisher was Scribner's. Fay, a convert to the

3. Mizener, *The Far Side of Paradise*, p. 75.

church, was jolly, witty, well-traveled, and entirely sophisticated. He was the model for Monsignor Thayer Darcy in *This
Side of Paradise*, and the strong attachment between Amory
and "Monsignor" was based on Fitzgerald's own relationship
with Fay.[4] Leslie for his part was thoroughly literary and exotic, especially to young Fitzgerald. He had attended Cam-
bridge, where he had known the poet Rupert Brooke—then
one of Fitzgerald's literary heroes. Fitzgerald had reviewed
two of Leslie's books with high praise in the *Nassau Lit* issues
for May and June 1917, and he had visited Leslie during the
fall of that year. In November 1917 he began corresponding with the older author about the details of the novel-in-
progress. This correspondence is preserved on both sides, and
it reveals much about the growth of *The Romantic Egotist* in
the months that followed.[5]

On 26 November Leslie, writing in response to a letter from
Fitzgerald, showed some confusion about what his young
friend was doing. "I shall be interested in your novel in verse—"
Leslie wrote, "it sounds bold!" He continued:

However there is no form of literature which should not
be attempted or concocted before the farce of the Anglo-
Celto-Latin civilisation is rung down.

4. For the best account of Fay's relationship with Fitzgerald, see Piper,
Critical Portrait, pp. 37–39, 46–48. See also Rev. R. C. Nevius, "A Note on
F. Scott Fitzgerald's Monsignor Sigourney Fay and his Early Career as an
Episcopalian," *Fitzgerald/Hemingway Annual 1971*, pp. 105–13.

5. Leslie's letters were saved by Fitzgerald and are now at Princeton University Library. They are quoted here with Leslie's kind permission. Leslie
published Fitzgerald's letters to him in the *Times Literary Supplement*,
6 Nov. 1959, p. 643. Other letters in this correspondence have been published
in *The Letters of F. Scott Fitzgerald*, ed. Andrew Turnbull (New York: Scribner's, 1963), pp. 371–79, and in *Correspondence of F. Scott Fitzgerald*, ed.
Matthew J. Bruccoli and Margaret M. Duggan (New York: Random House,

I wish you would stick to your idea of a book of poems. I was much interested in those you read to me at the Newman School. Thirty or forty would make a book or livret. Nobody has time to finish a book these days. They are served up scaffolding and design more than complete solid form.

It took almost a month for Leslie's letter to catch up with Fitzgerald in Kansas, but when he finally received it he wrote back to set Leslie straight about his plans and to reveal the title of his book-to-be:

> Dec 22 1917
> Ft Leavenworth Kan.

My dear Mr Leslie

Your letter followed me here—My novel isn't a novel in verse. It merely shifts rapidly from verse to prose but its mostly in prose.

The reason I've abandoned my idea of a book of poems is that I've only about twenty poems and cant write any more in this atmosphere—while I can write prose so I'm sandwitching the poems between rheams of autobiography and fiction. It makes a pot pourri especially as there are pages in dialogue and in vers libre but it reads as logically for the times as most public utterances of the prim and prominent. It is a tremendously concieted affair. The title page looks (will look) like this

THE ROMANTIC EGOIST
by
F. SCOTT FITZGERALD

1980), pp. 22–23, 28–29, 36–37, 66–67. All quotations from the Fitzgerald-Leslie correspondence in the discussion that follows are from these sources.

The Best is over
You may remember now and think and
                              sigh
Oh silly lover!"
                    Rupert Brooke

"Oll me coucha banga loupa
Domalumba guna duma . . ."
                    Gilbert Chesterton

"Experience is the name Tubby gives to all his mistakes"
                    Oscar Wilde

I'll send you a chapter or two to look over if you would.[6]

Leslie answered encouragingly on New Year's Day, 1918: "I like the idea of your book. Conceit is the soul or germ of modern literature and of course 'egotism' is the long sought synonym for 'style'. Send me any MS you wish criticised and I will rectify the spelling into the bargain though I presume 'spelling libre' must be the next step in literature."

6. Monsignor Fay may possibly have inspired the title. In a 10 Dec. 1917 letter to Fitzgerald, Fay suggested calling the novel "The Romance of an Egoist." Twelve days later, in his 22 Dec. letter to Leslie, Fitzgerald calls the novel *The Romantic Egoist*. In subsequent letters Fitzgerald and his correspondents refer to the book as either *The Romantic Egoist* or *The Romantic Egotist*. For instance, in Fitzgerald to Leslie, 22 Dec. 1917, it is "EGOIST" while in Fitzgerald to Wilson, 10 Jan. 1918, it is "EGOTIST"; but in Scribner's to Fitzgerald, 19 Aug. 1918, it is "Egoist" again. There seems to be no pattern governing the appearance of either form. The distinction between "egoist" and "egotist" has become blurred today, but in Fitzgerald's time an "egoist" was a confident, self-assured person, while an "egotist" was a conceited, boastful talker. Fitzgerald may or may not have been aware of this distinction: Stephen Palms is sometimes an "egoist" and at other times more of an "egotist," and so either title might be appropriate. Since Fitzgerald finally settled on "The Romantic Egotist" as the title for book 1 of *This Side of Paradise*, and since two of the surviving TS chapters of the early novel are entitled "The Egotist Up" and "The Egotist Down," it seems proper here to use *The Romantic Egotist*.

Fitzgerald worked steadily in Kansas. Conditions for writing there were bad, but he was able to overcome them. Almost three years later he recalled what it had been like to write a book in training camp.

> Every evening, concealing my pad behind Small Problems for Infantry, I wrote paragraph after paragraph on a somewhat edited history of me and my imagination. The outline of twenty-two chapters, four of them in verse, was made, two chapters were completed; and then I was detected and the game was up. I could write no more during study period.
>
> This was a distinct complication. I had only three months to live—in those days all infantry officers thought they had only three months to live—and I had left no mark on the world. But such consuming ambition was not to be thwarted by a mere war. Every Saturday at one o'clock when the week's work was over I hurried to the Officer's Club, and there, in a corner of a roomful of smoke, conversation and rattling newspapers, I wrote a one-hundred-and-twenty-thousand-word novel on the consecutive week-ends of three months. There was no revising; there was no time for it. As I finished each chapter I sent it to a typist in Princeton.
>
> Meanwhile I lived in its smeary pencil pages. The drills, marches and Small Problems for Infantry were a shadowy dream. My whole heart was concentrated upon my book.[7]

But Fitzgerald wrote this account in 1920 from a position of success. *This Side of Paradise* had made him famous—his efforts had paid off. In 1917 and 1918, it had not actually been

7. "Who's Who—and Why," p. 61.

that easy. More revealing of his difficulties are passages from *The Romantic Egotist* itself. Early in the first chapter, he admits:

> A week has gone here in the aviation school just hurried by with early rising by the November moon, and here I am with not one chapter finished—scrawled pages with no form or style—just full of detail and petty history. I intended so much when I started, and I'm realizing how impossible it all is. I can't re-write and all I do is form the vague notes for chapters that I have here beside me and the uncertain channels of an uneven memory. I don't seem to be able to trace the skeins of development as I ought. I'm trying to set down the story part of my generation in America and put myself in the middle as a sort of observer and conscious factor.
>
> But I've got to write now, for when the war's over I won't be able to see these things as important—even now they are fading out against the back-ground of the map of Europe. I'll never be able to do it again; well done or poorly. So I'm writing almost desperately—and so futily.[8]

A similarly hesitant, groping, apologetic tone is evident throughout the early parts of *The Romantic Egotist*. Young Fitzgerald was finding his first sustained act of composition more difficult than he had imagined, but even with these problems he was progressing quickly. By 10 January he had completed eighteen chapters and was optimistic enough to write this letter to Edmund Wilson:

8. Quoted from Matthew J. Bruccoli, *Some Sort of Epic Grandeur: The Life of F. Scott Fitzgerald* (New York: Harcourt Brace Jovanovich, 1981), p. 84.

THE ROMANTIC EGOTIST
by F. Scott Fitzgerald
". . . the Best is over
You may complain and sigh
Oh Silly Lover . . ."

Rupert Brooke

"Experience is the name Tubby gives to his mistakes."

Oscar Wilde

Chas. Scribner's Sons (Maybe!)

MCMXVIII

There are twenty-three chapters, all but five are written, and it is poetry, prose, *vers libre* and every mood of a temperamental temperature. It purports to be the picaresque ramble of one Stephen Palms from the San Francisco fire thru school, Princeton, to the end, where at twenty-one he writes his autobiography at the Princeton aviation school. It shows traces of Tarkington, Chesterton, Chambers, Wells, Benson (Robert Hugh), Rupert Brooke and includes Compton-Mackenzie-like love affairs and three psychic adventures including an encounter with the devil in a harlot's apartment.

It rather damns much of Princeton but it's nothing to what it thinks of men and human nature in general. I can most nearly describe it by calling it a prose, modernistic *Childe Harold* and really if Scribners takes it I know I'll wake some morning and find that the debutantes have made me famous overnight. I really believe that no one else could have written so searchingly the story of the youth of our generation.[9]

9. *Letters*, p. 323.

Fitzgerald's claims of rapid composition were apparently truth-
ful. By 4 February 1918 he could write to Shane Leslie that
"the first draft of *The Romantic Egotist* will be ready for your
inspection in three weeks altho I'm sending you a chapter
called 'The Devil' next week." Fitzgerald in fact sent Leslie
two chapters.

> Dear Mr. Leslie:
> Here's Chapter xvi "The Devil" and Chapter xiii I
> picked it out as a Chapter you could read without knowing
> the story. I wish you'd look it over and see what you think
> of it. It's semi-typical of the novel in its hastiness and
> scrubby style.

Leslie read the chapters and was intrigued. "Is it all like that?"
he wrote. "I think you have hit on *something*. You must come
and talk it all over with me."

In mid-February Fitzgerald completed training camp and
took a week's leave before joining his regiment at Camp Taylor,
Kentucky. He spent his leave time at the Cottage Club in
Princeton revising the remaining chapters of *The Romantic
Egotist*. On his way to Kentucky in early March he passed
through Washington, D.C., and delivered the finished typescript to Leslie, who was living there. After some delay Leslie
sent it to Charles Scribner on 6 May 1918 with this covering
letter:

> Dear Mr Scribner,
> I am sending you the MS of a book by a Princeton boy a
> friend of mine and a descendant of the author of the Star
> spangled banner. He calls himself the descendant of Bene-
> dict Arnold in his autobiography in the approved style of

modern youth! I have read it through and in spite of its disguises it has given me a vivid picture of the American generation that is hastening to war. I marvel at it's crudity and its cleverness. It is naive in places, shocking in others, painful to the conventional and not without a touch of ironic sublimity especially toward the end. About a third of the book could be omitted without losing the impression that it is written by an American Rupert Brooke. I knew the poetic Rupert Brooke and this is a prose one, though some of the lyrics are good and aparently original. It interests me as a boy's book and I think gives expression to that real American youth that the sentimentalists and super patriots are so anxious to drape behind the canvas of the Y.M.C.A. tent. Though Scott Fitzgerald is still alive it has a literary value. Of course when he is killed it will also have a commercial value. Before leaving for France he has committed it to me and will you in any case house it in your safe for the time? If you feel like giving a judgment upon it, will you call upon me to make any alterations or perform whatever duties accrue to a literary sponsor.

Without tying you down in any way, accept our best thanks in advance as well as my apology for intruding upon your good will yet again—

yours faithfully

Shane Leslie [10]

---

10. Two copies of this letter survive. The ribbon copy is in the Scribner Archive at Princeton University Library; a carbon copy, sent by Leslie to Fitzgerald, is in the Fitzgerald Papers. I have quoted the ribbon copy, which Leslie sent to Scribner's. Leslie apparently told Arthur Mizener that he corrected the spelling and grammar in *The Romantic Egotist* before forwarding it to Scribner's (see *The Far Side of Paradise*, p. 76). I can discover no documentary evidence to corroborate this statement. None of the extant fragments shows such corrective markings.

Leslie sent a copy of this letter to Fitzgerald, who responded gratefully:

> 45th Inf. Camp Gordon Ga.
> May 8th, 1918.

Dear Mr. Leslie,
Your letter filled me with a variety of literary emotions . . . you see yours is the first pronouncement of any kind that I've received upon my first born. . . .
That it is crude, incredibly dull in place is too true to be pleasant. . . . I have no idea why I hashed in all that monotonous drivel about childhood in the first part and would see it hacked out like an errant apendicitus without a murmer. . . . There are too many characters and too much local social system in the Princeton section . . . and in all places all through the verses are too obviously lugged in. . . .
At any rate I'm tremendously obliged for taking an interest in it and writing that awfully decent letter to Scribner. . . . If he thinks that a revision would make it at all practicable I'd rather do it than not or if he dispairs of it I might try some less conservative publisher than Scribner is known to be.

There was now little for Fitzgerald to do but wait. He fretted through the spring and summer of 1918 in anticipation of a decision. Perhaps subconsciously he knew that *The Romantic Egotist* had not been ready for submission, and he feared its rejection.

The delay on Scribner's part was caused by a division of opinion among its editors. The only one who liked *The Romantic Egotist* was Maxwell Perkins. Of the other editors Edward L. Burlingame called Fitzgerald's manuscript "hard sledding" and William C. Brownell was firmly against taking it.[11] Scribner's was a conservative, traditional publishing house. *The Romantic Egotist* was filled with garrulous adolescent narration and hyper-significant youthful experiences—hardly Scribner material. Perkins was enthusiastic about Fitzgerald's book, but he was only a junior editor and could not carry the day. He did, however, win a second chance for the young author. When Scribner's returned the manuscript to Fitzgerald more than three full months later, it was accompanied by an encouraging letter, very likely written by Perkins for the firm:

Aug. 19, 1918.

Lieutenant F. Scott Fitzgerald,
Hq. Co. 67th Infantry,
Camp Sheridan, Ala.

Dear Sir:

We have been reading "The Romantic Egoist" with a very unusual degree of interest;—in fact no ms. novel has come to us for a long time that seemed to display so much originality, and it is therefore hard for us to conclude that we cannot offer to publish it as it stands at present. Of course, in this we are considerably influenced by the prevailing conditions, including a governmental limitation on the number of publications and very severe manufacturing costs which make profitable publication far more difficult than ordinarily; but we are also influenced by certain characteristics of the novel itself. We generally avoid criticism as beyond our function and as likely to be for that reason not unjustly resented by an author but we should

11. Roger Burlingame, *Of Making Many Books* (New York: Scribner's, 1946), p. 67.

like to risk some very general comments this time because, if they seemed to you so far in point that you applied them to a revision of the ms., we should welcome a chance to reconsider its publication.

The chief of these is that the story does not seem to us to work up to a conclusion;—neither the hero's career nor his character are shown to be brought to any stage which justifies an ending. This may be intentional on your part for it is certainly not untrue to life; but it leaves the reader distinctly disappointed and dissatisfied since he has expected him to arrive somewhere either in an actual sense by his response to the war perhaps, or in a psychological one by "finding himself" as for instance Pendennis is brought to do. He does go to the war, but in almost the same spirit that he went to college and school;—because it is simply the thing to do. It seems to us in short that the story does not culminate in anything as it must to justify the reader's interest as he follows it; and that it might be made to do so quite consistently with the characters and with its earlier stages.

It seems to us too that not enough significance is given to some of those salient incidents and scenes, such as the affairs with girls. We do not suggest that you should resort to artificiality by giving a significance inconsistent with that of the life of boys of the age of the hero, but that it would be well if the high points were heightened so far as justifiable; and perhaps this effect could partly be gained by pruning away detail you might find could be spared elsewhere. Quite possibly all that we have said is covered by your own criticism of the ms, as at present a little "crude" and that the revision you contemplate will itself remove the basis of our criticism, and if when you make this you allow us a second reading we shall gladly give it.

We do not want anything we have said to make you think we failed to get your idea in the book,—we certainly do not wish you to "conventionalize" it by any means in either form or manner, but only to do those things which it seems to us important to intensify its effect and so satisfy a reader that he will recommend it,—which is the great thing to accomplish toward a success.

We know how busy you are and how absorbed you must be in your present work, and it is rather difficult to think of you as being able to do this revising too; but as you have yourself spoken of it we have less hesitation in making suggestions toward it and in sending back the ms;—we hope we shall see it again and we shall then reread it immediately,—in fact our present delay was due to a misapprehension which led us to think you did not care about an early decision.

Very truly yours,
Charles Scribner's Sons[12]

The warmth and courtesy of the rejection are striking, but equally so are two notes of criticism which in the end damned *The Romantic Egotist:* it was poorly organized, and it had no proper ending. This second criticism—that the story did not "culminate in anything"—lodged itself in Fitzgerald's mind and troubled him throughout subsequent efforts to make his work publishable. A little over a year later he remembered his dilemma: "How could I intrigue the hero into a 'philosphy of life' when my own ideas were in much the state of Alice's after the hatter's tea-party."[13] How to get the hero somewhere! How to bring the story to a definite conclusion when the hero's real

---

12. *Correspondence*, pp. 31–32.
13. Fitzgerald, "Preface to 'This Side of Paradise,'" *Fitzgerald/Hemingway Annual 1971*, p. 1.

life had only begun! Fitzgerald wrestled with this problem when he revised *The Romantic Egotist* for resubmission to Scribner's, and he tackled it again when he composed *This Side of Paradise*. Unfortunately he never solved it completely and never brought his book to a truly satisfactory conclusion.

Now, however, he was encouraged by the letter to begin revising immediately. Leslie gave him good advice: "Revise the book carefully," he wrote on 8 September. "It is not until one gets into one's literary stride that one ever dares to disregard publishers' injunctions." Fitzgerald apparently worked with care, but from the extant evidence it is impossible to tell just how much he did to the novel or how he did it. Did he revise his first typescript and have it freshly retyped? Did he add handwritten revisions to his existing typescript? Or did he revise selectively and have only portions retyped? Surviving ribbon-copy fragments of *The Romantic Egotist* are lightly reworked in black ink; these changes may represent rewriting done in the late summer of 1918. A large body of fragmentary work survives, but in no instance are there two typescripts, original and revised, of the same material. The surviving documents may all be from the revised version, but there is no way to test that possibility. It would have been nearly impossible for Fitzgerald to have had a fresh typescript of the entire novel prepared between mid-August 1918, when it was first rejected, and September, when the revised version went back to Scribner's. Just what the firm saw the second time is therefore a mystery, but whatever they saw they did not like, and again *The Romantic Egotist* was turned down. At Fitzgerald's request Perkins sent the book to several less conservative publishers, but they were not interested.[14] The manuscript came home to its discouraged author in October 1918.

14. Burlingame, *Of Making Many Books*, p. 67. On this same page, Burlingame writes that Fitzgerald revised his material from first to third person at

All was not gloomy, however. In July while Fitzgerald had been stationed near Montgomery, Alabama, he had met Zelda Sayre. Their relationship deepened through the impatient summer and the discouraged winter that followed. To his later regret Fitzgerald did not go overseas: when he was about to embark for Europe, the Armistice was signed. Discharged from military service in February 1919, he began making serious plans for marriage to Zelda. To a failed writer this meant finding work. Fitzgerald went to New York City and took a job as a copy-writer with the Barron Collier Advertising Agency, where he attempted to be a success in business by day and wrote commercial fiction on the side at night. But his advertising work bored him and paid little, and his record as a freelance author was poor. A few of the stories he sent to magazines were new, but most were old *Nassau Lit* efforts warmed over or short stories carved from the carcass of *The Romantic Egotist*. Nearly everything was rejected. That spring was not wasted, however: material from the new stories found its way into *This Side of Paradise*, and, more important, Fitzgerald learned that hastily done work could not make the grade on the New York market. Professional writing on that level was a full-time business.

So, evidently, was romancing Zelda. The distance between Fitzgerald in New York and his fiancée in Montgomery put a strain on their relationship that was too great. This pressure, compounded by Fitzgerald's failures at business and writing, led to a breakup in June 1919. Fitzgerald drowned his considerable sorrows on an epic drinking spree and quit his advertis-

---

Perkins's suggestion. (Both the original and the revised *Romantic Egotist* were primarily in first-person narration, but *This Side of Paradise* employs a third-person narrator.) No document exists to support Burlingame's statement, but Perkins was alive when *Of Making Many Books* was written, and Burlingame could have acquired this information from him.

ing job. Early in July he decided to stake everything on his novel and returned home to St. Paul. As he put it eighteen years later, the novel was his "ace in the hole."[15] He had determined, for the time being at least, to be a writer.

15. "Early Success," quoted from the critical text in "Notes on the Text of F. Scott Fitzgerald's 'Early Success,'" *Resources for American Literary Study* 3 (1973):94.

2

The Romantic Egotist

When Fitzgerald returned to St. Paul in July 1919, he carried with him the typescript of *The Romantic Egotist*. Only fragments survive today. According to Fitzgerald the finished typescript consisted of either twenty-two or twenty-three chapters, four of them in verse; but all that remain today are six complete chapters, one of which is in verse, and fragments large and small of at least six more chapters.[1] In 1920 Fitzgerald wrote that the typescript had been 120,000 words long, but this figure was probably inaccurate—Fitzgerald was certainly approximating and likely exaggerating.[2] What survives today totals only about fifty-four thousand words. Perhaps half of *The Romantic Egotist* is missing, but the extant fragments still give a good indication of the nature and contents of the novel.

The most important surviving fragments are the Donahoe typescripts. In October 1918 Fitzgerald sent five typescript chapters of *The Romantic Egotist* to his school friend Charles "Sap" Donahoe who, like Fitzgerald, was serving in the Army. Donahoe and Fitzgerald had attended Newman School at the same time and had remained friends through their years together at Princeton. Donahoe, in fact, was a character (named "Tump") in *The Romantic Egotist*. Donahoe forgot to return

1. Fitzgerald to Edmund Wilson, 10 Jan. 1918, in *Letters*, p. 323, puts the number at twenty-three chapters, but "Who's Who—and Why," p. 61, gives the count as "twenty-two chapters, four of them in verse."
2. "Who's Who—and Why," p. 61.

the chapters and in 1948, when the revival of interest in Fitzgerald was beginning, he unearthed them and sent them to
Arthur Mizener. Through Mizener the fragments made their
way to Princeton and today are kept in the Fitzgerald Papers.

One cannot be certain about the provenance of any of the
five chapters. Differences in paper size, stock, and watermark,
and in carbon-copy freshness and color, indicate that no two
chapters were typed at the same time. Chapter I was done on a
typewriter different from the one used to type the other four
chapters. Each chapter is uniform within itself, but no two
chapters match in all physical aspects.[3] The five chapters
(numbered I, II, V, XII, and XIV) may be working drafts from
the first version of *The Romantic Egotist*, or copies from the
second version, or a mixture of both. These chapters could be
early or late—there is no sure way to tell. One fact, however,
is certain: they are rejected drafts. Fitzgerald sent them to
Donahoe while the revised *Romantic Egotist* was at Scribner's. Whatever materials he had on hand at that point were
left over and discarded.[4]

Chapter I, entitled "The Egotist Up," opens with the first-
person narrator of *The Romantic Egotist*, Stephen Palms, addressing the reader from aviation training camp. Like many
other soldiers of his time, Fitzgerald was caught by the romance and glamour of World War I flyers. One remembers the
youthful William Faulkner, who trained for the Royal Cana-
dian Air Force in 1918 and who incorporated some of those
experiences into his fiction. But Faulkner actually knew something about flying and had firsthand information about the
air corps. Fitzgerald knew nothing about military aviation.

3. For physical characteristics of the surviving fragments of *The Romantic
Egotist*, see Appendix A of this study.
4. The envelope in which Fitzgerald sent the chapters to Donahoe is post-
marked 14 Oct. 1918, from Montgomery, Ala. A covering note mentions that
the revised version of the novel is at Scribner's.

Whether his ignorance hampered him is not known, since none of the surviving fragments deals with flight or aerial combat.

What these drafts do deal with, almost to a fault, is Stephen Palms. Except for a few details, Stephen is closely based on Fitzgerald himself, much more so than Amory Blaine will later be. Stephen's narrative is so painfully open and naive that it is difficult to read without a curious discomfort, at once effective and annoying. After looking over some of these early drafts, Monsignor Fay, in a letter to Fitzgerald, commented on his "brutal frankness in the use of the first person." But, Fay continued, "there is always something far more arresting about a self revelation than there is about a story told about somebody else."[5]

Stephen begins his first chapter with a long, self-conscious preamble in which he addresses the reader directly:

> I am informed that the time has come for a long rambling picaresque novel. . . . I shall ramble and be picaresque. I shall be intellectual and echo H. G. Wells, and improper like Compton Mackenzie. . . . My form will be very original for it will mingle verse and prose and not be vers libre; and this interest the new poets. . . . Anyway, this is an autobiography which begins in vagueness, passes slowly through clarity and ends up in the filmy mist of an aviation school. . . . I'd better proceed or I'll be giving away my climax in the beginning like H. G. Wells.[6]

In this first chapter Fitzgerald charts Stephen's adolescence from early years in San Francisco through a middle period in Minneapolis. Chapter 1 is almost formless: it consists of inci-

---

5. Fay to Fitzgerald, 17 Aug. 1918, *Correspondence*, p. 30.
6. Piper, *Critical Portrait*, p. 50.

dent after incident, detail after detail, from Stephen's early life. The wealth of material is impressive, but there is little clear organization or effective presentation. Fitzgerald was having difficulty with his opening chapter, and he knew it. In passages throughout the narrative he breaks in and apologizes for the lack of form, and these sections create an interesting authorial perspective. Fitzgerald was writing hastily and revising little; he was pressed for time and was working under poor conditions. He would therefore occasionally stop and explain his method—or lack of method—to an imaginary reading audience. Fitzgerald appears to have been addressing these passages as much to himself as to his future readers. He was attempting to work out a narrative perspective as he wrote and trying to explain and apologize for his poor organization.

Stephen Palms's early life closely parallels Amory Blaine's. Like Amory, Stephen comes from a wealthy family. His father dies, and he and his mother, Catherine, go on a pilgrimage from hotel to hotel through the United States, just as Amory and his mother, Beatrice, will do in *This Side of Paradise*. Money runs low and Stephen and his mother and brother move to Minneapolis to live with his mother's sister. There Stephen goes through some of the same experiences that Fitzgerald will later give to Amory, though Stephen's upbringing is by-and-large more conventional. There are minor love affairs with girls at dancing classes and adolescent musings on popularity and success in sports.[7]

Stephen, the "romantic egotist," is much interested in himself. He presents this lengthy analysis of his own inner makeup:

> I had a definite philosophy which was a sort of aristocratic egotism. I considered that I was a fortunate youth

7. Some of the incidents are similar to material in Fitzgerald's "Thought-

capable of expansion to any extent for good or evil. I based this, not on latent strength, but upon facility and superior mentality. I thought there was nothing I could not do, except, perhaps, become a mechanical genius; still I traced special lines in which I considered [I] must excell, even in the eyes of others. *First:* Physically—I marked myself handsome; of great athletic *possibilities*, and an extremely good dancer. Here I gave myself about eighty percent. *Second:* Socially—In this respect, my condition was, perhaps, most dangerous, for I was convinced that I had personality, charm, magnetism, poise, and the ability to dominate others. Also I was sure that I exercised a subtle fascination over women. *Third:* Mentally—Here I was sure that I had a clear field in the world. I was vain of having so much, of being so talented, ingenuous and quick to learn.

To balance this I had several things on the other side. *First:* Morally—I thought I was rather worse than most boys, due to latent unscrupulousness and the desire to influence people in some way, even for evil. I knew I was rather cold; capable of being cruel; lacked a sense of honor, and was mordantly selfish. *Second:* Psychologically—Much as I influenced others, I was by no means the 'Captain of my Fate.' I had a curious cross section of weakness running through my character. I was liable to be swept off my poise into a timid stupidity. I knew I was 'fresh' and not popular with older boys. I knew I was completely the slave of my own moods, and often dropped into a surly sensitiveness most unprepossessing to others. *Third:* Generally—I knew that at bottom I lacked the es-

book," an adolescent journal he kept during 1910 and 1911. See *Thoughtbook of Francis Scott Key Fitzgerald*, intro by John R. Kuehl (Princeton: Princeton University Library, 1965).

sentials. At the last crisis, I knew I had no real courage, perseverance or self-respect.

So you see I looked at myself in two ways. There seemed to have been a conspiracy to spoil me and all my inordinate vanity was absorbed from that. All this was on the surface, however, and liable to be toppled over at one blow by an unpleasant remark or a missed tackle; and underneath it, came my own sense of lack of courage and stability. If I may push it farther still, I should say that, underneath the whole thing lay a sense of infinite possibilities that was always with me whether vanity or shame was in my mood.[8]

Such obviously autobiographical passages are fascinating to the student of Fitzgerald's life, but they are not successful as fiction. Fitzgerald had not yet adopted the cynically objective attitude he would employ in *This Side of Paradise*. Not all of the passages in this chapter are so studiously self-absorbed, however. In other sections Fitzgerald displays a good eye for detail, and set pieces like this one stand out:

These sleighrides. . . . Nowhere but in Minnesota had they such sleighrides. It would be three when we set out in thick coats and sweaters, the girls flushed and consciously athletic; and boys slightly embarassed but rakish in jumping off and on with complete abandon, to a chorus of little shrieks of simulated anxiety. At a dusky five o'clock we'd reach our destination; usually a club, and have hot chocolate and chicken sandwiches and a dance or two by the graphophone. Then the dark and the crisp frost would come down outside and Mrs. Hollis, or Mrs. Campbell or Mrs. Wharton would take the boy who had frozen his

8. Quoted from Andrew Turnbull, *Scott Fitzgerald* (New York: Scribner's, 1962), pp. 34–35.

cheeks on the way out, home in her limousine, while the rest of us loitered on to the verandah and waited for the sleighs under the pale January moon. On the way out the girls always sat together, but going back things were different. Then there were mixed groups of four and six, and more than occasionally, of two; and the only unmeltable elements were at the front of the sleigh where the cross-eyed girl talked with painful concentration to the chaperon and in the back where the half dozen shy boys lurked and whispered and pushed each other off.[9]

But such passages are infrequent in this first chapter. Taken together "The Egotist Up" is rambling and boring; it does not catch and hold the reader's attention, as a first chapter must.

More particularly, there is a fundamental confusion in Stephen's character. We are told that he is a child of wealth—precocious, well traveled, sophisticated, and educated by tutors—but as soon as his hotel-to-hotel pilgrimage through America is finished he immediately adapts to Minneapolis and almost overnight becomes a typical middle-class boy. There is no period of adjustment, no gradual change in personality. Stephen's behavior in Minneapolis does not match his background. This same fault mars Amory's character, but with Stephen the defect is more pronounced. The problem was that Fitzgerald was trying to create a composite character. Later in his career this technique would be one of his strongest: Dick Diver in *Tender Is the Night*, for example, is a composite based on several real-life persons—Walker Ellis, Theodore Chanler, Gerald Murphy, and Fitzgerald himself, to name the four major models.[10] But the skill and smoothness with which Fitzgerald synthesized Dr. Diver's personality is not evident in Ste-

9. Turnbull, *Scott Fitzgerald*, pp. 23–24.
10. See chapter 2 of Matthew J. Bruccoli, *The Composition of* Tender Is the Night (Pittsburgh: University of Pittsburgh Press, 1963).

phen's character. Fitzgerald was trying to create a hero with a glamorous, exotic background who could also play scenes from his own childhood and adolescence in St. Paul. He accomplished this by clumsily grafting Stephen's Minneapolis experiences onto some early years of travel and sophistication. The effect was to bifurcate Stephen's personality. This same problem causes trouble with Amory Blaine: Fitzgerald never quite decided who or what Amory was, and so there are many Amorys in *This Side of Paradise*, no two of whom are exactly alike. As we shall see, there are several reasons for the fragmentation of Amory's personality. At this point one need only note that the problem already exists in Amory's predecessor, Stephen Palms.

The opening chapter of *The Romantic Egotist* is not successful as fiction, but it makes good reading for students of Fitzgerald's later work. Into Stephen's narrative Fitzgerald crowded a great amount of material, most of it autobiographical. For *This Side of Paradise* he salvaged the best of these scenes and discarded the rest, but not permanently. Throughout his career he drew repeatedly on these experiences for short stories and essays. In a brief five-paragraph passage, for instance, one finds the germ of "Absolution," a 1924 short story that Fitzgerald later said was a discarded opening to *The Great Gatsby*.[11] In "Absolution" a young boy named Rudolph Miller goes to confession. Asked by the priest if he has told any lies he replies proudly, "Oh, no, Father, I never tell lies." Immediately Rudolph realizes that he has committed a terrible sin by in fact telling a lie in confession. His terror for his soul, fueled by Catholic dogma and parental disapproval, is quite real. The story is one of Fitzgerald's best, but the early version in *The Romantic Egotist* is not at all memorable—it is merely one incident among many. Stephen thinks of his lie in confes-

11. "Absolution," *American Mercury* 2 (June 1924); collected in *All the Sad Young Men* (New York: Scribner's, 1926).

sion as a good speech that he would not have missed making; he admits that the experience kept him awake many nights, but he now regards it as trivial and amusing.

This same callow tone pervades Stephen's picture of his father. Stephen remembers when he and his father would walk downtown in their best clothes every Sunday, and he describes his father's highly developed class sense and fine southern manners. This episode was reused twice: first in the important essay "The Death of My Father," unpublished during Fitzgerald's lifetime, and later in *Tender Is the Night* where Dick Diver muses over the profound influence his father, recently deceased, has had on his own personality. In *The Romantic Egotist*, the treatment is flippant and cynical. Stephen has no sense of the meaning behind his father's polished manners; he sees them merely as social tricks which one can use to impress adults. When Fitzgerald reworked this material years later he had outgrown his youthful attitudinizing and was able to fashion, from his father's legacy, a probing autobiographical essay and a moving section of *Tender Is the Night*.[12]

Other material from "The Egotist Up" found its way into *This Side of Paradise*, and still other incidents were resurrected years later for the Basil Duke Lee stories, published in the *Saturday Evening Post* in 1928 and 1929.[13] The first chapter of *The Romantic Egotist* is an unsuccessful beginning for a novel, but it preserves early texts of important material that Fitzgerald would draw on for the rest of his career.

Chapter II, "The Egotist Down," is the story of Stephen's first half-year at Markle Prep School. He arrives full of high

12. "The Death of My Father" first appeared in *Princeton University Library Chronicle* 12 (Summer 1951). A facsimile of the original manuscript of the essay is included as an appendix to *The Apprentice Fiction of F. Scott Fitzgerald*, ed. John Kuehl (New Brunswick: Rutgers University Press, 1965).

13. The Basil stories have been collected in *The Basil and Josephine Stories*, ed. Jackson R. Bryer and John Kuehl (New York: Scribner's, 1973).

hopes for social and athletic success but ruins his chances by being fresh and by being cowardly at football. He becomes the school pariah, miserable and unhappy. This chapter is fairly well organized. It is at least a true "chapter" from Stephen's life rather than a mass of experiences scattered over several years. There is development—Stephen is at first hopeful, later unhappy, finally despairing—and there is some sense of form. The incidents in "The Egotist Down" are not, however, as lively and vivid as those in "The Egotist Up." For example, Stephen tells of an English class during which the school's star halfback lets loose several frogs on the floor. The boys in the class are all in on the joke, and they leap onto their seats and desks, shrieking in mock terror, much to the consternation of the cross-eyed instructor. The material is amusing enough, but Stephen's narrative is so insistently "funny" that the humor falls flat.

As with the first chapter, however, certain passages catch the eye of the reader familiar with Fitzgerald's later fiction:

Christmas came at last and as the train drew out of Chicago and struck the cool, crisp air of Wisconsin, my heart rose in the joy of homecoming. Three weeks of comfort and friendliness and even sentiment were before me, I thought. No one at home knew about my life at Markle. I had written nothing of the state of things to the family, it would have horrified me that they should know. My vanity would not have allowed it. When next morning the familiar buildings and the exhilarating cold of Minneapolis flooded into my consciousness from the chilly observation platform of the train where I lingered hungrily, I felt Markle drop its cloudy weight from my mind like a bad dream.[14]

14. Piper, *Critical Portrait*, p. 153.

This mental image of returning home to the midwest at Christmas after a fall term at an eastern prep school would remain in Fitzgerald's mind. Later it would blossom into the beautifully evocative passage in *The Great Gatsby* where Nick Carraway remembers his own train trip home at Christmas.[15]

When Fitzgerald assembled *This Side of Paradise* he excluded most of the material from "The Egotist Down," making Amory's unhappy first year at prep school a minor stage in his development. The only scenes salvaged were "Incident of the Well-Meaning Professor" and "Incident of the Wonderful Girl." In the rejected material, however, one again finds situations, such as a fistfight between Stephen and another boy on the Markle baseball diamond, which Fitzgerald used later for the Basil Duke Lee stories.

The third surviving chapter is entitled, with a characteristic Fitzgerald misspelling, "Spires and Gargoiles." It tells of Stephen's freshman year at Princeton, and the first part is good. Here Stephen describes the sophomore "rushes" and dissects the Princeton social system in great detail. He observes and records well; in one memorable passage he compiles a careful list of undergraduate slang, defining such words as *smelt* (a girl), *nudo* (mentally deficient), *stroke* (to kiss), and *scut* (a person of the lower order). The narrative, though disjointed, is colorful and humorous—reminiscent of boys' books like Owen Johnson's *Stover at Yale* (1912), an early favorite of Fitzgerald's and later a "textbook" for Amory.

The first half of "Spires and Gargoiles" is effectively done, but attached to the end of the chapter is a curious third-person account of an unnamed student, apparently Stephen, sweating through a final exam. Whether or not the student stays in Princeton depends on his passing the course. Fortunately he gets through. Fitzgerald took this sequence from his own

15. *The Great Gatsby* (New York: Scribner's, 1925), pp. 211–12.

short story "The Spire and the Gargoyle," published in the *Nassau Lit* for February 1917. He simply lifted large sections from the story, with third-person point-of-view unchanged, and dropped them into this chapter of *The Romantic Egotist*. The result is thoroughly to confuse the narrative. There is no good artistic reason for retaining third-person point-of-view, since Stephen himself narrates the rest of the chapter. Fitzgerald's motive was probably expedience: he was in a hurry to finish the chapter and did not take time to rework this material in first-person narration. In *This Side of Paradise* he would retain only the best passages from the story—the memorable descriptions of the Princeton campus, with its symbolic Gothic architecture and its brooding spirit of beauty mixed with struggle and aspiration.

This difficulty with point-of-view is important, for it is the first hint of a problem that will cause trouble later in *This Side of Paradise*. At this early stage in his development, Fitzgerald evidently did not understand about narrative point-of-view in fiction. In mature stories like "The Rich Boy" and novels like *The Great Gatsby*, Fitzgerald would show true mastery of point-of-view, but in composing *The Romantic Egotist* he seems not to have realized the disorienting effect of an abrupt shift in narrative viewpoint. In both *The Romantic Egotist* and *This Side of Paradise*, Fitzgerald created many problems by reusing old material without thoroughly rethinking and rewriting it in the new point-of-view. "Spires and Gargoiles," with its third-person ending, is but the first example.

Nearly all of the material in this chapter reappears in *This Side of Paradise*. Two large sections—Amory's first meeting with Thomas Parke D'Invilliers and the early stages of their friendship, and Dick Humbird's death—were salvaged and reused. Smaller incidents also reappear: Amory's first trip to the Princeton movies, the pranks at 12 University Place, and Amory's analysis of his middle-class social position in college.

The early sections of *This Side of Paradise*, particularly the first two chapters, bear no truly close resemblance to what survives of *The Romantic Egotist;* but as the published novel progresses, worked-over material from the earlier book appears with increasing frequency. Much of "Spires and Gargoiles" was incorporated into *This Side of Paradise*, and the last two Donahoe chapters, numbered XII and XIV, were merged completely into the book. Chapter XII, entitled "Eleanor," is an early version of the chapter "Young Irony" in *This Side of Paradise*. Fitzgerald reworked the material, but this early version is still similar to the chapter in the published novel. Two noteworthy sections, not in *This Side of Paradise*, survive in the Donahoe chapter. The first is a discussion of Rupert Brooke and what his poetry meant to Fitzgerald's generation. Brooke is important to *This Side of Paradise*, for the novel owes much, including its title, to the English poet. Eleanor and Stephen take him as an artistic ideal: Eleanor writes poetry in the Brooke manner, and Stephen imitates Brooke's attitudes and literary postures. Both characters see the poet as a rebel against Victorian standards, a heroic unbeliever.[16]

The second excluded section describes a chilling encounter with the supernatural. Stephen and Eleanor, waiting to go to a dance, are sitting in Eleanor's library. Eleanor has had a heavy fur coat brought down for the evening; she has placed it on a sofa and has turned an electric fan toward it to drive away the odor of moth balls. Eleanor is in a curious mood—dull, heavy, and unusually affectionate. Suddenly the coat begins to *crawl* over the sofa toward the couple. They freeze with terror as it creeps toward them like a furry jellyfish. The description is extremely repellent. Finally the crawling stops; a maid enters and Eleanor tells her to take the coat away. After a moment of

16. See Robert Roulston, "*This Side of Paradise:* The Ghost of Rupert Brooke," *Fitzgerald/Hemingway Annual 1975*, pp. 117–30.

instinctive hesitation the maid removes the coat, and Stephen and Eleanor are no longer afraid.

This strange episode reinforces the connection in *This Side of Paradise* between sex and the supernatural. The reference is muted, but Eleanor's intense, affectionate mood has something to do with sex, perhaps with the female menstrual cycle. Similar encounters with supernatural presences occur three times in the published text of *This Side of Paradise*, and all three have sexual overtones. Fitzgerald tried to retain the episode of the crawling fur coat in *This Side of Paradise*. Evidence from the manuscript shows that he revised the scene heavily and even attempted to rewrite it completely before deciding, in a late stage of revision, to cut it from the book altogether.

Of the five chapters that Fitzgerald sent to Donahoe, the text of chapter xiv, "The Devil," is closest to the corresponding part of *This Side of Paradise*. In fact this Donahoe chapter is the carbon of the ribbon typescript that Fitzgerald eventually cut, revised, and incorporated into the manuscript as "The Devil," "In the Alley," and "At the Window." These subchapters describe Amory's encounter with the devil in a chorus girl's apartment. Fitzgerald took eight of the twelve ribbon-copy sheets of the material, revised them heavily, and included them in the manuscript as pages 291, 295, 296, 302, 303, 306, 307, and 308. He bridged the gaps between typed sheets with fresh handwritten pages. The four missing typescript sheets, which still survive in the Donahoe carbon, bear material condensed or cut in revision. The only noteworthy segment omitted was a two-page sequence in which Stephen, back at his hotel the day after he has encountered the devil, calls the hotel doctor for help but becomes exasperated and angrily orders the man from his room. The brief scene was superfluous, and Fitzgerald cut it.

The fragments that most clearly show the close relationship

between *The Romantic Egotist* and *This Side of Paradise* are the fifty-four typescript sheets from the earlier novel that Fitzgerald spliced into the manuscript of the later one. These sheets identify additional parts of the published book that originated in *The Romantic Egotist*. Amory's affair with Isabelle, for instance, was pieced together from two episodes, the first involving a similar character named Isabelle and the second involving a girl named Rosalind—but not the same Rosalind Connage who will appear later in *This Side of Paradise*. Amory's trip to Deal Beach came from *The Romantic Egotist*, as did his midnight bicycle ride to Lawrenceville with Tom D'Invilliers. The episodes in Mr. Rooney's make-up class and the scene in which Amory receives his blue failure slip both came from the earlier typescript. Amory's "personality/personage" discussion with Monsignor Darcy, along with most of the Burne Holiday material and the short sequence on ghost-exorcism, all were salvaged from this typescript, as was the poem beginning "Good-morning, Fool . . . ," originally a complete verse chapter. Finally, both the long section on Amory's cousin Clara and the passage in which he composes a poem to the Victorians came from *The Romantic Egotist*.

The smallest and least important surviving fragment of *The Romantic Egotist* is the *Smart Set* text of Fitzgerald's short story "Babes in the Woods." Fitzgerald first published the story in the *Nassau Lit* for May 1917, and it saw print twice more: in the *Smart Set* for September 1919 and as "Isabelle" and "Babes in the Woods," two subchapters in *This Side of Paradise*. The episode was also part of *The Romantic Egotist*, but only five typescript leaves of that version survive. They are among the fifty-four sheets described in the paragraph just above. Collation of the *Smart Set* text with the unrevised text of these typescript leaves (that is, with the typed text before Fitzgerald added handwritten revisions) proves the two texts almost identical. And the principal characters in the *Smart Set* version are named Stephen Palms and Isabelle. The rejected and discarded typescript pages therefore were probably very close to the corresponding passages in the *Smart Set* text. But this discovery is not especially significant, because there are almost no important textual differences among any of the extant versions of the "Babes" material—*Nassau Lit, Romantic Egotist, Smart Set,* or *This Side of Paradise.* The "Babes" section was simply a block of fiction that Fitzgerald transferred to suit his purposes: from short story to novel, back to short story, and back again to novel.

Of more interest is the fact that the *Romantic Egotist* text, like the other three versions, is narrated from Isabelle's point of view—third-person limited omniscient narration centering on her consciousness. Again Fitzgerald has incorporated old *Nassau Lit* material, with point-of-view unchanged, into the first-person-narrated *Romantic Egotist,* just as he had done earlier with "The Spire and the Gargoyle." How skillfully he blended this new shift into his story is a mystery, since the first few pages of the *Romantic Egotist* "Babes" do not survive. Still, it is safe to say that yet another change in point-of-view must have confused further the already puzzling narrative technique of the novel. Fitzgerald obviously had not yet learned to manipulate point-of-view.

The extant fragments of *The Romantic Egotist* total some fifty-four thousand words, but in 1920 Fitzgerald estimated that the novel had been much longer. From the evidence, however, it is impossible to discover just what the rest consisted of. In a 4 September 1919 letter to Maxwell Perkins, Fitzgerald identified one more *This Side of Paradise* subchapter—"Ha-Ha Hortense!"—as having originated in the earlier book. Beyond this point, one cannot be sure.

One can, however, engage in some limited speculation. *The*

Romantic Egotist almost certainly contained much material based on Fitzgerald's friendship with Monsignor Fay. A deleted passage, still readable on one of the revised typescript sheets, gives a hint about this lost material. In the passage, the priest—here named Dr. Taylor—mentions a school friend of Stephen's who is absent from *This Side of Paradise*. The reference hints of an intimate three-way camaraderie among the priest, Stephen, and Stephen's friend. Fitzgerald's relationship with Fay in real life had included another Newman School boy named Stephan Parrott; a fictional version of their three-way relationship must have figured in *The Romantic Egotist*. Indeed Stephen Palms apparently took his Christian name from Stephan Parrott.[17] Other sections undoubtedly dealt with Stephen's upperclass years at Princeton, but only small fragments of this material have survived. Likewise there is no extant text that deals with Stephen's military experiences, though the later chapters of *The Romantic Egotist* must have covered them.

The surviving materials, though limited, still give a good idea of the nature of *The Romantic Egotist*. The book was

17. There was in addition a student at Newman School named Charlie Palms, and it is possible that Fitzgerald took his fictional character's name from this person. (See Fay to Fitzgerald, 30 June 1918, Fitzgerald Papers.) Piper, in *Critical Portrait*, p. 46, gives an inaccurate account of the naming of Fitzgerald's hero. He writes that the central character in the early novel was first named "Michael Fane," after the hero of Compton Mackenzie's *Youth's Encounter*, and was later called "Stephen Fitzfay," a combination formed from the names of Stephan Parrott, Fitzgerald, and Fay. Piper gives a general citation to the entire Fitzgerald-Fay correspondence for support of his statement, but close reading of these letters, particularly of two dated 4 Oct. 1917 and 10 Dec. 1917, reveals that "Michael Fane" was a nom de plume employed by Fitzgerald on some early writing, and that "Stephen Fitz Fay" was a name with which both Fitzgerald and Fay signed their letters to one another. There is no hard evidence to indicate that the hero of *The Romantic Egotist* was ever named anything but Stephen Palms.

immature in thinking and ragged in form, and its narrative technique was badly handled. John Peale Bishop, to whom Fitzgerald sent sections of the typescript for criticism, wrote Fitzgerald a telling analysis of the novel. He compared it to *Youth's Encounter*, by the English author Compton Mackenzie:

> Now to come to your own book. Scott, I think if you will recollect the volume above [*Youth's Encounter*], or the account of Wells' youthful heroes, or Anatole France's *Le Livre de Mon Ami*, the glaring defect of your book will be noted. I have a theory that novels as well as plays should be in scenes. The marvellous effect of *Crime and Punishment* is largely due to the cumulative effect of the successive climaxes. Each scene—chapter what you will should be significant in the development either of the story or the hero's character. And I don't feel that yours are. You see Stephen does the things every boy does. Well and good. I suppose you want the universal appeal. But the way to get it is to have the usual thing done in an individual way. You don't get enough into the boy's reactions to what he does. Its the only way to awaken the meaning which is the real source of pleasure in boy's stories for grown-olds. . . . Think of Michael Fain's reaction to the iron bars of his crib. It's wonderful. Now your boy sleds, but I don't *feel* that he enjoys sledding. In matter of fact, I don't realize fully that he does sled. You see what I mean? Each incident must be carefully chosen—to bring out the typical: then ride it for all its worth.[18]

Bishop hits on two major weaknesses of *The Romantic Egotist*—lack of selectivity and failure to highlight key inci-

18. Bishop to Fitzgerald, Jan. 1918, *Correspondence*, p. 25.

dents. These defects probably resulted from the hasty composition of the novel, and they were shortcomings that Fitzgerald recognized and admitted. But *The Romantic Egotist* was an impressive first attempt: it is similar in many ways to *This Side of Paradise*, sharing with it not only scenes and characters but also a precociousness and vitality that together compensate for many of its technical failings. Some of the best material in the published novel was plundered from *The Romantic Egotist*: the chilling encounter with the devil in Phoebe's apartment, the "young aesthete" scenes with Tom D'Invilliers, and the amusing, skillfully portrayed confrontations between Amory and Isabelle. Some of the weakest sections also come from the earlier typescript: the windy discussions between Amory and Burne Holiday and the emotionally overwrought "Young Irony" chapter, for example. *The Romantic Egotist* was the product of a talented but not yet fully developed mind. Fitzgerald had plenty of good material—more, in fact, than he could handle—but he had still to learn that personal experience must be objectified and thoroughly reimagined if it is to be made into successful fiction. He himself would put it this way in 1926, not long after publication of *The Great Gatsby:* "Material, however closely observed, is as elusive as the moment in which it has its existence unless it is purified by an incorruptible style and by the catharsis of a passionate emotion."[19] These two elements—incorruptible style and passionate emotion—were lacking in *The Romantic Egotist*. Scribner's was undoubtedly right in rejecting the novel, especially since the rejection spurred Fitzgerald on to compose *This Side of Paradise*, a better book.

19. "How to Waste Material—A Note on My Generation," *Bookman* 63 (May 1926):262–65.

"Babes in the Woods," *Nassau Literary Magazine,* May 1917. Stylistic revision for *The Romantic Egotist.*

"The Debutante," *Nassau Literary Magazine,* January 1917. Revised heavily for *Smart Set.*

The Romantic Egotist (1917–18). Scenes, characters, and incidents from *The Romantic Egotist* were reused extensively in *This Side of Paradise.* Fifty-four sheets from the typescript of the novel were heavily revised and incorporated into the manuscript of *This Side of Paradise.*

"Babes in the Woods," *Smart Set,* Sept. 1919. Very lightly revised from the *Romantic Egotist* text.

"The Débutante," *Smart Set,* Nov. 1919. Revised lightly and incorporated into Book II, Chapter I, of *This Side of Paradise.*

"Young Irony." Short story extracted from the *Romantic Egotist* typescript; rejected by *Scribner's Magazine,* June 1919. Eight sheets of this version were revised and used in *This Side of Paradise.*

"The Spire and the Gargoyle," *Nassau Literary Magazine,* Feb. 1917. Sentences and phrases are used in "A Damp Symbolic Interlude" in Book I, Chapter II, of *This Side of Paradise.*

"Princeton—The Last Day," *Nassau Literary Magazine,* May 1917. Used as a prose poem on the last page of Book I of *This Side of Paradise.*

"On a Play Twice Seen," *Nassau Literary Magazine,* June 1917. Used in Book I, Chapter IV, of *This Side of Paradise.*

"Sentiment—and the Use of Rouge," *Nassau Literary Magazine,* June 1917. A few sentences and phrases are used in Book II, Chapter V, of *This Side of Paradise.*

"The Cameo Frame," *Nassau Literary Magazine,* Oct. 1917. A stanza from this poem is rendered into prose in Book I, Chapter IV, of *This Side of Paradise.*

THIS SIDE OF PARADISE
(Working title: *The Education of a Personage.*)

3

The Education of a Personage

Early in July 1919 Fitzgerald returned from New York to his parents' home in St. Paul. His spirits were low: he had failed at business and at writing, and his relationship with Zelda had ended—apparently forever. "I retired not on my profits but on my liabilities," he recalled in 1937, "which included debts, despair and a broken engagement and crept home to St. Paul to 'finish a novel.'"[1] Thus began a cyclical pattern of success/ failure/comeback that characterized much of his later life. In future years he would hit other personal, professional, and financial lowpoints, and after desperate struggles would recover from most of them. In fact one can argue convincingly that Fitzgerald needed the stimulus of impending disaster to make him write, since in times of tranquility and security he usually produced little. When he was brought low, however, he found in his difficulties the resources for excellent fiction. That is the background for *The Great Gatsby* and *Tender Is the Night*, and also for *This Side of Paradise*.

In that summer of 1919 Fitzgerald thought of his novel as a chance to win two all-important things—success and love. These two desires were inextricably bound together in his mind, because for him success was impossible without the golden girl. Under these powerful, self-imposed pressures Fitzgerald delivered, just as he would so often do in later life. He wrote the novel, placed it with a prestigious house, saw it

1. "Early Success," p. 94.

succeed, won the girl, and made a name for himself in literature. This real-life Horatio Alger story became central to Fitzgerald's conception of his own life, and to the fiction that grew
out of it. As he later wrote, "The compensation of a very early
success is a conviction that life is a romantic matter. In the
best sense one stays young."[2]

Fitzgerald climbed to the attic of his parents' house and set
up shop. He proceeded methodically, first pinning an outline
of chapters to his curtain. He worked long hours, and his parents brought up sandwiches and milk so he would not have to
stop for meals. They even screened his telephone calls so he
would not be disturbed.[3] Fitzgerald labored from early July
until late August 1919. The result of that concentrated burst
of work was the complete manuscript of a novel. He was
now calling it *The Education of a Personage*, but he would
change the title once more—to *This Side of Paradise*.[4] This
manuscript preserves, on every page, complicated and fascinating evidence about the composition of the novel. It reveals
much about Fitzgerald's working habits and helps explain the
strengths and shortcomings of the published book.

The manuscript is a complex document. It contaihs 635
leaves, numbered consecutively. The numbering, however, is
irregular. Sheets inserted late in the compositional process are
half-numbered (pages 74½ and 263½, for example) or are
marked with number-letter combinations such as 408A–
408B–408C. Other sheets are marked to combine pagination
(20+21+22 and 506+507); these numberings compensate for
material cut from the manuscript at some late stage.

2. "Early Success," p. 98.
3. Turnbull, *Scott Fitzgerald*, pp. 97–98.
4. When he was a boy Fitzgerald had met Henry Adams. The title *The
Education of a Personage* may have been suggested by Adams's *The Education of Henry Adams*. Thornton Hancock in *This Side of Paradise* is based on
Adams.

Most of the leaves are holograph drafts. Fitzgerald wrote with lead pencils in a flowing, rounded, open script that is easily legible. He used three pencils alternately: one had a light, hard lead with a purplish cast, another had a regular black No. 2 lead, and the third had a soft black lead that resembled charcoal. It is possible almost to look over his shoulder as he wrote, to watch him lay down a pencil with a work-blunted tip and pick up one with a freshly sharpened point. Some leaves, in fact, were written with a recurring succession of pencils that become increasingly blunt, as if Fitzgerald, into a hot stint of composition, were reluctant to stop even to sharpen his writing instruments.

While the stack of holograph leaves grew, the supply of clean paper diminished. Up to and including leaf 243, the leaves are white wove paper measuring 215 × 279 millimeters, every fourth leaf usually watermarked "HAMMER-MILL | BOND." After leaf 243, the bond paper was used up, and Fitzgerald switched to a coarse wove unwatermarked paper measuring 217 × 281 millimeters.

The manuscript contains many heavily revised typescript sheets, some of them ribbon copies and some carbons. There are numerous pages from the *Romantic Egotist* typescript along with typed pages from a play, a short story, and several poems. Writing and typing is on the rectos of all leaves except for brief false starts on a few versos. The typed sheets are revised in black or blue ink or in black pencil. Fitzgerald wrote directions to his typist in the margins, and nearly every page is slashed through with a pencil mark, the typist's indication of having copied that sheet.[5]

Fitzgerald must have begun with vigorous resolve to rewrite the novel afresh from start to finish. At the beginning, even passages he took directly from *The Romantic Egotist* are

5. For a full description of the manuscript, see Appendix B of this study.

redrafted in longhand. He was often working with text from the old typescript, but he resisted the temptation to do a cut-and-paste job and instead wrote out brand new drafts. This method was sound. There is a difference between revising an existing typescript and drafting a fresh handwritten version. A typescript resists change; the determination to revise soon melts before the fixed verbal form and sequence on the paper. New thoughts must be made to fit between old ones, and a thoroughgoing revision is impossible. A fresh longhand draft, by contrast, takes its form as it goes. Its development is not hampered by an existing text. Even if the author is working with a previous version at his elbow, as Fitzgerald was doing here, he is free to expand, condense, add, delete—and to re-think. By preparing fresh drafts of the early sections, Fitzgerald was able to reconsider everything, from single words to entire scenes. He cut out weak incidents from *The Romantic Egotist*, expanded the remaining material, and rewrote thoroughly. The resulting first chapter succeeds: it captures the reader's curiosity and encourages him to continue.

Midway through the second chapter, however, Fitzgerald realized that it was taking too much time to write out fresh drafts. He therefore decided to take old sheets from the *Romantic Egotist* typescript and splice them into the manuscript.[6] This was a crucial shift in tactics. Fitzgerald was no longer rewriting; he was now merely revising. The typed sentences on these leaves had originally been composed at least eighteen months before, and some of them even dated back to his junior year at Princeton. He had developed and matured so rapidly that many of these old typed sentences were very much inferior to the fresh handwritten sentences he was now

6. Page 197, the first typescript leaf in the manuscript, begins with "the shifting search-light" at 70.19 of the first edition. For correspondences between manuscript leaves and the printed first edition, see Appendix C.

producing. The old dialogue, especially, was less effective than the new. Fitzgerald improved those old typescripts by revision and tinkering, but he was unable to refine out all of their weaknesses.

By recycling old typescript, Fitzgerald also caused problems with the ordering of his scenes. When an author composes each scene in fresh holograph, he develops a sense, a "feel," for the ebb and flow of the work. His characters' moods and emotions must not shift abruptly without good reason; their attitudes must instead change gradually, and the reader must be prepared for these shifts. When an author is working with blocks of old typescript, however, he often finds it hard to recapture this feeling, and he is likely to juxtapose old scenes awkwardly. This is exactly what happened when Fitzgerald assembled chapter 2. In a chillingly realistic section near the end of the chapter, Amory witnesses the bloody death of Dick Humbird in a car accident. The scene is eerie and scary, full of foreboding and mystery. Humbird has been an ideal of sorts for Amory, who is profoundly shocked by his sudden realization that human life is impermanent. But the very next night Amory is happily fox-trotting at the Spring Prom with Isabelle, having entirely forgotten Humbird's terrible death—or so we are expected to believe. Humbird's death does not taint Amory's weekend with Isabelle; he watches admiringly as the stags cut in on her with "joyous abandon," and he is eager to make this night "the centre of every dream."[7] The two scenes, both salvaged from *The Romantic Egotist* typescript, jar against each other badly. There is no transition between Amory's shocked grief one night and his ingenuous puppy love the next. Fitzgerald was determined to reuse both scenes, and

7. *This Side of Paradise* (New York: Scribner's, 1920), pp. 96–97. Subsequent quotations from this edition will be cited parenthetically in the text.

so he simply dropped them next to one another in his new manuscript, made a few revisions, and forged on.

Even more interesting is the effect that these revised typescript sheets had on point-of-view. In *The Romantic Egotist*, as we have seen, Fitzgerald had cavalierly mixed old writing narrated in the third person with new writing narrated in the first person. Something similar happened when he began weaving old typescript sheets into his manuscript. *The Romantic Egotist* had a first-person quasi-autobiographical narrator; the new novel had a third-person omniscient narrator. Consequently Fitzgerald had to do some extensive plastic surgery. He did the work carefully, and the resulting prose reads smoothly—on the surface. Inevitably, though, Fitzgerald's incorporation of sheets from the earlier novel into this new manuscript affected narrative tone. Stephen Palms had been an intensely personal and sensitive narrator with a painfully serious attitude. The third-person narrator of the new novel, by contrast, is world-weary, ironic, even cynical. This shift in tone is not surprising; it reflects changes that had taken place in Fitzgerald's own disposition. Much had happened to him: he had left college without taking a degree, gone through a disappointing stint in the Army, written a first novel that he could not publish, and fallen for a girl who would not marry him. It is hardly surprising that the new, omniscient narrator is more skeptical about Amory than Stephen Palms had been about himself. The narrative tone in book 1 of the novel is therefore mixed—an imperfect blend of the blasé with the naive.

Stephen Palms's open, boyish point of view is apparent in passages that originated in the *Romantic Egotist* typescript, but Stephen's self-conscious tone is undercut and contradicted in the fresh holograph sections. For instance, the narrator's attitude toward Amory's upbringing, in the early holograph pages of the new manuscript, is highly ironic. Stephen had not been nearly so cynical about his early years, but by completely rewriting these sections in longhand Fitzgerald was able to introduce the new slant. Again, Amory's reaction to his father's death is cynical, even disrespectful. Not surprisingly this scene was done in fresh handwritten draft. By contrast, in the section dealing with campus rebel Burne Holiday, Fitzgerald tired of rewriting and spliced in ten pages of old typescript. As a result the narrator's attitude here is basically Stephen's, transferred to the third person, but still wide-eyed and immature. Fitzgerald even preserved a discussion of why Amory (actually Stephen) was still afraid of the dark.

This is a notable example of how an author's techniques of composition can affect scenes, characters, and narrative point-of-view in his fiction. The old typescript leaves from *The Romantic Egotist* cause point-of-view in book 1 of the new novel to be an odd mixture, and this variation affects Amory's character. When the text derives from fresh handwritten drafts, one sees the new Amory—spoiled, pampered, and experienced (if not matured) beyond his years. But when the text derives from the old typescripts, one sees an Amory who is only a slightly altered version of Stephen Palms, a boyish young pup. This mixture confuses many readers. Just how seriously is one to take Amory in book 1? In some scenes the third-person narrator regards him with a healthy dose of irony; in others this same narrator seems unaware of the immaturity and foolishness of Amory's behavior. The manuscript shows that this problem was caused when Fitzgerald incorporated old typescript sheets from *The Romantic Egotist* into his new novel.

Fitzgerald was probably unwise to use these typescripts, but still it is instructive to watch him transform old material into new. Two long sections from the second chapter provide good examples. In the first section, Amory and his friends go to the beach for a weekend of pranks and fun. In *The Romantic Egotist* the action and dialogue had been divided equally among Stephen's friends, with each one contributing to the humor and joking. The narrative, as a result, was diffuse and directionless; it should have been entitled "Sophomore Fun." In the new manuscript Fitzgerald pulled the scattered bits together by making Kerry Holiday master of ceremonies. With Alec Connage as his sidekick, Kerry thinks up the escapades and does the talking; the rest of the group goes along for the ride. This rearrangement of roles is effective. The reader watches Kerry, just as the characters do, and wonders what mischief he will think up next. With this shift, though, Fitzgerald inevitably altered the relationships among the characters. He knew it and used it. In a fresh holograph bridge passage, added between the typescript sheets, he set down the new status of each person:

> Amory was content to sit and watch the by-play, thinking what a light touch Kerry had, and how he could transform the barest incident into a thing of curve and contour. They all seemed to have the spirit of it more or less, and it was a relaxation to be with them. Amory usually liked men individually, yet feared them in crowds unless the crowd was around *him*. He wondered how much each one contributed to the party, for there was somewhat of a spiritual tax levied. Alec and Kerry were the life of it, but not quite the centre. Somehow the quiet Humbird, and Sloane, with his impatient superciliousness, were the centre. [P. 85.]

This is an excellent example of how Fitzgerald, at his best, could transform old material into new.

Just as adept is his merging of Isabelle and Rosalind from *The Romantic Egotist* into one character—Isabelle of the new novel. The old Isabelle in the earlier typescript is similar to the new Isabelle, but she drops out of the story after meeting Stephen at the dance in Minneapolis. Rosalind from *The Romantic Egotist* is an entirely different character; she is not the same Rosalind who will appear in the new novel. Fitzgerald used typescript sheets that dealt with both girls. He kept the introductory episode with Isabelle largely intact but borrowed his ending from the old Rosalind material. There are only five typescript sheets that deal with the old Rosalind; they reveal little about her personality and nothing about how she met Stephen. They record only his long, dreamy letter to her, the events of their prom weekend together, and her first kiss with him, ruined a few seconds later when his shirt-stud presses against her pretty neck. Fitzgerald merged Isabelle and Rosalind together easily and gracefully; there is no jarring, probably because both characters were based on the same person— Ginevra King, Fitzgerald's first serious sweetheart. Only the manuscript reveals that the new Isabelle was once two separate persons.

All of the major episodes in chapter 2, and many of the minor ones, are drawn from the *Romantic Egotist* typescript. Only the opening scenes, with Amory arriving in Princeton, meeting Kerry, and watching the marching singers, and three of the later subchapters—"Historical," "Descriptive," and "Carnival"—are totally new.

Chapter 3, "The Egotist Considers," is concerned with loss: Amory loses his infatuation with Isabelle, his chances for success in college, his father, and some of his financial security. This chapter again mixes old typescript with fresh holograph. The new material concerns the death of Mr. Blaine, the discussion of his estate, the letters from Beatrice and Monsignor to Amory, and the budding poet Tanaduke Wylie. The last page of "The Egotist Considers" (page 308 of the manuscript) preserves interesting evidence about the structure of *This Side of Paradise*. In the published book, this chapter ends with the terrifying devil section, and the next chapter begins with a description of Burne Holiday. In the manuscript, however, there is no chapter break—only a new subchapter. Fitzgerald divided the original third chapter in some postmanuscript stage, probably in typescript. Apparently he had been revising and splicing so quickly that he lost his sense of proportion and put two chapters' worth of material into one.

In chapter 4, or what became chapter 4 between manuscript and print—Fitzgerald salvaged as much remaining typescript from *The Romantic Egotist* as he possibly could. The section is a catchall for Stephen's Princeton experiences, plus the Clara episode, also from *The Romantic Egotist*, plus bits and pieces of new material. Not surprisingly this chapter is uneven, and Amory's behavior is inconsistent. His moods fluctuate from gloomy to bright, melancholy to optimistic.

For chapter 4 he salvaged the long-winded discussions between Amory and Burne about Marx, Tolstoy, and the superiority of blue-eyed blonds—thus preserving ten pages of sophomoric narrative that he might well have cut. There are a few amusing new incidents like Burne's weekend with Phyllis Styles, the intercollegiate prom-trotter, but well over half the chapter is recycled from *The Romantic Egotist*. One cannot tell how closely Fitzgerald was working from existing typescript when he drafted the handwritten parts of the chapter, but the only sections completely in holograph are brief: the taxicab trick on the dean, the Phyllis Styles episode, the scene involving the Bible quotation in the *Princetonian*, and the comments on World War I.

Book 1 of the new novel is largely a collection of fragments taken, in one way or another, from *The Romantic Egotist* and from Fitzgerald's *Nassau Lit* writings. He had begun well, but in his impatience he had rushed ahead, splicing and improvising as he went along. In one sense this was good: it saturated the manuscript with people, places, and action. As Fitzgerald said later, the four chapters are *"crowded* (in the best sense)."[8] But while these chapters contain most of the best writing done by Fitzgerald since he entered Princeton, they are finally not successful. Most of the individual scenes are good, and some are excellent, but they are not effective as parts of an integrated novel.

Fitzgerald realized that. When he looked back over the mass of material in book 1, he saw that he had serious trouble: the book was in danger of collapsing. There was so much incident and so little clear plot line and controlling idea that his new novel was open to the same charge that had been leveled at *The Romantic Egotist*—the protagonist was not going anywhere. But by this time the section was finished, its material assembled and ordered, and its hardpressed author impatient to move along. Fitzgerald needed a quick solution, a way to pull the material together without going back and rewriting again.

He found that solution. He wrote two fresh pages which, when inserted into the manuscript, threated a wire through the bits and pieces of narrative and jerked them into line. These pages were unquestionably afterthoughts: they are half-numbered and are written on paper different from the holograph sheets that surround them. The first passage, on page 104½ of the manuscript, is this short paragraph:

He was changed as completely as Amory Blaine could ever be changed. Amory plus Beatrice plus two years in Min-

---

8. Fitzgerald to Perkins, 16 Aug. 1919, in *Dear Scott/Dear Max: The Fitzgerald-Perkins Correspondence*, ed. John Kuehl and Jackson R. Bryer (New York: Scribner's, 1971), p. 18.

neapolis—these had been his ingredients when he entered St. Regis'. But the Minneapolis years were not a thick enough overlay to conceal the "Amory plus Beatrice" from the ferreting eyes of a boarding-school, so St. Regis' had very painfully drilled Beatrice out of him, and begun to lay down new and more conventional planking on the fundamental Amory. But both St. Regis' and Amory were unconscious of the fact that this fundamental Amory had not in himself changed. [P. 35.]

In the second inserted passage, on page 263½ of the manuscript, Fitzgerald develops the thought:

Amory's point of view, though dangerous, was not far from the true one. If his reactions to his environment could be tabulated, the chart would have appeared like this, beginning with his earliest years:

1. The fundamental Amory.
2. Amory plus Beatrice.
3. Amory plus Beatrice plus Minneapolis.

Then St. Regis' had pulled him to pieces and started him over again:

4. Amory plus St. Regis'.
5. Amory plus St. Regis' plus Princeton.

That had been his nearest approach to success through conformity. The fundamental Amory, idle, imaginative, rebellious, had been nearly snowed under. He had conformed, he had succeeded, but as his imagination was neither satisfied nor grasped by his own success, he had listlessly, half-accidentally chucked the whole thing and become again:

6. The fundamental Amory. [Pp. 108–9.]

The improvisation was effective. Partly because Fitzgerald had changed his working methods, and partly for other reasons, the major problem in book 1 is the inconsistency of Amory Blaine. Of course there is inconsistency inherent in his personality: that, after all, is the point of the novel—to trace the development of such a young man. But just as troubling is the inconsistency in the narrator's attitude toward Amory. Are we to view Amory literally or ironically? He is sharply in focus through chapter 1 and most of chapter 2, but thereafter his character becomes increasingly diffuse. By inserting these two passages at the last minute, Fitzgerald was attempting to explain away the confusion.

The two passages suggest that Fitzgerald himself had only lately, and suddenly, begun to understand the character he had created. The two sheets introduce into the novel the concept of "the fundamental Amory"—the self that must be recognized, accepted, and revealed. In one sense this concept was an explanation of Amory's inconsistent behavior, but in another sense the idea came from a leap in Fitzgerald's perceptions. He had apparently come to terms with what it meant to be young, posing, and growing painfully, and to that extent his late revising was successful. His hero, at least, was going somewhere.

But where was Amory going? The major historical event of recent times was World War I, but Fitzgerald's war experience had been limited. He had seen no combat, had not even gone overseas. He had passed through just an interlude in his life. For writers like Ernest Hemingway, John Dos Passos, and E. E. Cummings, the war had cataclysmic significance; for Fitzgerald its events were small and personal, the most meaningful of which was finding Zelda. But his novel was pegged to reality, and so Fitzgerald had to account for this period in Amory's life.

What Fitzgerald did was to follow book 1 with "Interlude: May, 1917–February, 1919." This brief section contains three wartime documents—a letter from Monsignor to Amory, a poem written by Amory, and a letter from Amory to Tom D'Invilliers. Fitzgerald was attempting to convey by omission what he was not equipped to communicate otherwise—the effects of war on his hero. This expedient was only partly successful. Later in the novel we are told that Amory has led troops in combat, but the experience seems to have affected him little. His eventual disillusionment is rooted more in his disappointment with American life and in his loss of Rosalind than it is in the terrors of battle. Amory's wartime experiences are therefore reduced to something small, almost petty.

Another of Fitzgerald's expedients was more successful. In the Interlude he adapted reality to fictional purposes by "borrowing." Manuscript page 378, a typescript sheet, seems at first to be another page from *The Romantic Egotist*, but closer examination shows that it originated elsewhere. It bears the text of Monsignor Darcy's poetic keen, "A Lament for a Foster Son, and He going to the War Against the King of Foreign." As it turns out, Fitzgerald actually lifted the page from one of Monsignor Fay's letters and put it right into the manuscript. He kept the rest of the letter; it too is at Princeton in the Fitzgerald Papers. The typed characters and paper stock of Fay's letter (dated 10 December 1917) exactly match the typing and paper of manuscript page 378, thus identifying beyond question the origin and authorship of the poem. Fitzgerald's use of Fay's poem is not an adaptation; it is a direct steal.

Fitzgerald incorporated other passages from Fay's letters into Monsignor Darcy's letters to Amory. Fitzgerald explained the process to Shane Leslie:

> It seems a pity that something even more exhaustive can't be written about Dr. Fay. He always told me to save his let-

ters and some day we'd all publish them anonymously in some form. I found, however, that he'd written me less than he thought so the three letters that occur in the book are largely pieced together and even considerably added to from memories of remarks he'd made to me plus even a few things I thought he might have said.[9]

Comparison of the letters in the novel with Fay's actual letters shows how Fitzgerald worked. Below is a passage from Fay's 10 December 1917 letter to Fitzgerald:

How magnificent Streeter is. It gave me a frightful shock when you wrote me he thought me splendid. How can he be so deceived? Splendid is exactly the one thing that one of three is. We are many other things—we're extraordinary, we're clever, we could be said I suppose to be brilliant. We can attract people, we can make atmosphere, we can almost always have our own way, but splendid—rather not. . . . I am going to Rome with a wonderful dossier, and there will be "no small stir" when I get there. How I wish one of you were with me. This sounds like a rather cynical letter. Not at all the sort that a middle aged clergyman should write to a youth about to depart for the wars. The only excuse is that the middle aged clergyman is talking to himself. There are deep things in us and you know what they are as well as I do. We have great faith, and we have a terrible honesty at the bottom of us, that all of our sophistry cannot destroy, and a kind of childlike simplicity that is the only thing that saves us from being downright wicked.[10]

9. Fitzgerald to Leslie, 16 Nov. 1920, *Letters*, p. 378.
10. "Streeter" in the first sentence of this quotation is Henry Strater, who led a student movement to abolish Princeton's club system while Fitzgerald was there. Burne Holiday of *This Side of Paradise* is modeled on Strater. Fay's letter is published in *Correspondence*, pp. 23–24.

For the novel Fitzgerald reworked Fay's wording, but the fictional letter is still very similar to the real one:

> Do you remember that week-end last March when you brought Burne Holiday from Princeton to see me? What a magnificent boy he is! It gave me a frightful shock afterward when you wrote that he thought me splendid; how could he be so deceived? Splendid is the one thing that neither you nor I are. We are many other things—we're extraordinary, we're clever, we could be said, I suppose, to be brilliant. We can attract people, we can make atmosphere, we can almost lose our Celtic souls in Celtic subtleties, we can almost always have our own way; but splendid—rather not!
>
> I am going to Rome with a wonderful dossier and letters of introduction that cover every capital in Europe, and there will be "no small stir" when I get there. How I wish you were with me! This sounds like a rather cynical paragraph, not at all the sort of thing that a middle-aged clergyman should write to a youth about to depart for the war; the only excuse is that the middle-aged clergyman is talking to himself. There are deep things in us and you know what they are as well as I do. We have great faith, though yours at present is uncrystallized; we have a terrible honesty that all our sophistry cannot destroy and, above all, a childlike simplicity that keeps us from ever being really malicious. [P. 172.]

Fitzgerald took material from others besides Fay. Parts of *This Side of Paradise* came directly from Shane Leslie's letters, and other passages were taken from Zelda's letters and from her diary, which she allowed Fitzgerald to read and transcribe while they were engaged.[11] In transforming fact to fiction, however, Fitzgerald often changed the original source significantly. One of Leslie's letters demonstrates this point. Monsignor Fay died in January 1919, and Leslie went to his funeral. Fitzgerald was in the Army and could not attend, and so Leslie wrote him on 16 January to describe the ceremony:

I was ill my self and could not see him at the end but I crawled to the funeral, which he would have loved. It was magnificently Catholic and liturgical. Bishop Shahan sang solemn High Mass and Cardinal Gibbons gave the final absolutions. Bp Russell, Fr Sanderson, Delbos, Mrs Maloney, Fr Sargent, Fr Dolan were there and a host of friends and priests. I have been a week realising that his death was one of the sorrows of my life. His friendship was the choice find of my American years and I felt I had really settled down to a golden friendship such as only can be enjoyed by converts in the Church of their love and interest. But the inexorable shears have cut through all the threads which he had gathered into his hands. To me it was a haunting grief to see him lying in his coffin with closed hands upon his purple vestments. His face had not changed and as he never knew he was dying he shewed no pain or fear. It was just our dear old friend and the church was full of Newman people and all our friends with daft staring faces. The Cardinal looked the most stricken of all for as he said he was now left alone. It was a beautiful sight to see him like an Archangel in cope and mitre sprinkling the holy water while the choir sang the Requiem eternam.[12]

11. See Nancy Milford, *Zelda: A Biography* (New York: Harper and Row, 1970), pp. 35, 41, 44–46, and 55. The letters by Zelda from which Fitzgerald borrowed are published in *Correspondence*, pp. 42–45.

12. *Correspondence*, p. 36.

Fitzgerald's description of Monsignor Darcy's funeral is based on Leslie's letter but is heightened and intensified:

> Amory kept thinking how Monsignor would have en-
> joyed his own funeral. It was magnificently Catholic and
> liturgical. Bishop O'Neill sang solemn high mass and the
> cardinal gave the final absolutions. Thornton Hancock,
> Mrs. Lawrence, the British and Italian ambassadors, the
> papal delegate, and a host of friends and priests were
> there—yet the inexorable shears had cut through all these
> threads that Monsignor had gathered into his hands. To
> Amory it was a haunting grief to see him lying in his
> coffin, with closed hands upon his purple vestments. His
> face had not changed, and, as he never knew he was dy-
> ing, it showed no pain or fear. It was Amory's dear old
> friend, his and the others'—for the church was full of
> people with daft, staring faces, the most exalted seeming
> the most stricken.
>   The cardinal, like an archangel in cope and mitre,
> sprinkled the holy water; the organ broke into sound; the
> choir began to sing the *Requiem Eternam*. [P. 286.]

By incorporating such materials into his fiction, Fitzgerald did not endear himself to the people from whom he borrowed. Leslie, either as a private joke or as a subtle reprimand, quoted the cribbed funeral description in his review of *This Side of Paradise*.[13] And Leslie was unhappy over the passages taken from Fay's letters. He wrote Fitzgerald: "If you published Fay's letters you ought not to have put his name in the frontispiece"—meaning that Fitzgerald should not have dedicated the book to Fay.[14] Zelda appears not to have minded the bor-

13. *Dublin Review* (Oct., Nov., Dec. 1920), pp. 286–93.
14. Leslie to Fitzgerald, 3 Sept. 1920, *Correspondence*, p. 67.

rowings at first, but two years later in a spoof review of Fitzgerald's second novel, *The Beautiful and Damned*, she wrote, "Mr. Fitzgerald—I believe that is how he spells his name—seems to believe that plagiarism begins at home."[15]

Fitzgerald's borrowing habits have become an issue of debate, even a biographical cause célèbre. One Fitzgerald biographer has even argued that Zelda was the better writer and that Fitzgerald stole his best material from her. Certainly their dispute over *Save Me the Waltz* and *Tender Is the Night*, in which Fitzgerald made free use of materials from Zelda's mental breakdown but denied her the same privilege, is emotionally charged. Some day the whole question of Fitzgerald's borrowings from Zelda and from others, and of his collaborations with her and with others, should be investigated by a careful analysis of extant documentary evidence. Then perhaps Fitzgerald scholars will be able to speak accurately and not emotionally about the matter.

The question of borrowings in this novel is not crucial, since true verbal cribs are few. Nor does the question of morality seem significant. The morality or immorality of Fitzgerald's borrowing habits has no bearing on this novel as a work of fiction. Fitzgerald was after pure emotional intensity, and he was ruthless about using material from anyone's life, including his own, to achieve it. When he incorporated the words of others into his fiction, those words became his own work. Right, wrong, moral, or immoral, the words became Fitzgerald's property, inextricably tied in with what he wanted his novel to be. The borrowed words are as much parts of the book as are the passages composed entirely by Fitzgerald.

When Fitzgerald began book 2 of his novel he was faced

15. "Friend Husband's Latest," *New York Tribune*, 2 Apr. 1922; repr. *F. Scott Fitzgerald in His Own Time: A Miscellany* (Kent, Ohio: Kent State University Press, 1971), pp. 332–34.

with new problems. In book 1 he had simply reworked the best parts of *The Romantic Egotist* and had arranged them chronologically. Book 2, by contrast, would involve fresh invention, since by now nearly all of the salvageable material from *The Romantic Egotist* had been used up. Fitzgerald would have to break new ground, work up new characters, bring his novel to a close, and get his hero somewhere.

One problem that Fitzgerald faced was fictional time. In book 1 and the Interlude, he had covered nearly all of Amory's life—the first twenty-two and one-half years. In book 2 he had only the remaining nine months to work with, from February 1919 when Amory met Rosalind until November when he took his final walk to Princeton. Fitzgerald would have to work over this material thoroughly and extract its full fictional value, and this meant a change in method. In book 1 he had not been much concerned with continuity. Rather, he had assembled a large collection of incidents and had blocked them into four rough chapters. These chapters are not true fictional units but are instead approximate chronological groupings; Amory's life is presented as a series of brief scenes and not as a connected sequence. In book 2 Fitzgerald would have to abandon this undisciplined method and write true chapters—blocks of fiction that would fit into the novel and develop the hero's personality.

When Fitzgerald reworked "The Débutante"—the first chapter in book 2—he was in good form. His job was not easy because he had decided to incorporate the typescript of a play into his novel—no mean trick, since he would be mixing drama and fiction. Fitzgerald carried off the operation successfully, though, and got book 2 off to a strong start.

The initial section of this first chapter originated as a one-act play entitled "The Debutante," published in the *Nassau Lit* for January 1917. Fitzgerald revised the play while he was in

New York during the spring of 1919 and sold it to the *Smart Set*, where it appeared in November. He had submittted the ribbon typescript of the play to the magazine, but he had kept a carbon copy. In composing the chapter for *This Side of Paradise* he simply took this carbon and incorporated it into his manuscript.[16] Fitzgerald was taking a chance: in 1919 the use of drama dialogue in a novel was a radical innovation. Yet his instinct was right—the experiment works because Rosalind and Amory are actors playing roles. Fitzgerald used drama dialogue in only the first and last scenes of the chapter. In the first scene (salvaged from the *Smart Set* carbon), Rosalind and Amory fall in love; in the last scene (done in fresh holograph draft), they end their affair. During these two scenes they are posing and acting, and the drama dialogue and stage directions are appropriate. In the middle sections, however, they are truly in love, and Fitzgerald uses prose here to show that their words are natural and genuine. This alternation of drama dialogue and prose is highly effective, an admirable unity of form and content.

The creation of Rosalind, the most arresting female character in the novel, is a fascinating process. The *Nassau Lit* version of "The Debutante" had been based on Fitzgerald's romance with Ginevra King. The female lead, whose name is Helen, is not particularly striking; she is hardly more than a rich, spoiled little girl. The *Smart Set* version, however, was written after Fitzgerald had fallen in love with Zelda—indeed, while they were engaged—and as a result the heroine (now named Rosalind) is a more alluring mixture of Helen from the

16. Textual evidence confirms that Fitzgerald was using the *Smart Set* carbon. The unrevised text of the carbon matches the *Smart Set* text, and erased typed text on the carbon matches printed text in the *Smart Set*. In the upper left hand corner of the first page of the carbon, Fitzgerald's spring 1919 New York City return address is typed.

Nassau Lit and Zelda from real life. But by the time Fitzgerald revised the *Smart Set* carbon for the novel, Zelda had broken off her romance with him. Consequently, his depiction of Rosalind in the published novel blends his love and longing for Zelda with his bitterness over her decision not to marry him. Rosalind in *This Side of Paradise* was thus created by two separate revisions of, or additions to, the original female lead in the drama.

The passages below demonstrate the point. In the *Nassau Lit* version, the play opens with Helen center-stage, looking in a mirror:

> In the very middle of the confusion stands a girl. She is the only thing in the room which looks complete, or nearly complete. She needs to have her belt hooked, and has too much powder on her nose; but aside from that, looks as though she might be presented to almost anything at almost any time; which is just what is going to happen to her. She is terrifically pleased with herself and the long mirror is the focus of her activity. Her rather discontented face is consciously flexible to the several different effects. Expression number one seems to be a simple, almost childish, ingenue, upward glance, concentrated in the eyes and the exquisitely angelic eyelashes. When expression number two is assumed, one forgets the eyes and the mouth is the center of the stage. The lips seem to turn from rose to a positive, unashamed crimson. They quiver slightly—where is the ingenue? Disappeared. Good evening Sapho, Venus, Madam Du—no! ah! Eve, simply Eve! The pier-glass seems to please. Expression number three:—Now her eyes and lips combine. Can this be the last stronghold? The aesthetic refuge of womanhood; her lips are drawn down at the corners, her eyes droop and almost fill with tears. Does her face turn paler? Does—

No! Expression one has dismissed tears and pallor, and again—[17]

In the *Smart Set* version Fitzgerald keeps his heroine offstage until about a third of the way through the opening scene. Then he gives her this carefully prepared entrance in which one recognizes her as a version of young Zelda Sayre:

> Rosalind enters, dressed—except for her flowing hair. Rosalind is unquestionably beautiful. A radiant skin with two spots of vanishing color, and a face with one of those eternal mouths, which only one out of every fifty beauties possesses. It is sensual, slightly, but small and beautifully shaped. If Rosalind had less intelligence her "spoiled" expression might be called a pout, but she seems to have sprung into growth without that immaturity that "pout" suggests. She is wonderfully built, one notices immediately, slender and athletic, yet lacking underdevelopment. Her voice, scarcely musical, has the ghost of an alto quality and is full of vivid instant personality.[18]

For his new novel Fitzgerald added, as a long holograph insert among the carbon typescript sheets, a new and even more elaborate entrance for his female lead. The passage, which has become famous as a blueprint for the Fitzgerald heroine, contains many details that one associates with Zelda. In fact Fitzgerald took parts of the passage from one of her letters. The description is memorable enough to quote in full:

> And now ROSALIND enters. ROSALIND is—utterly ROSA-
> LIND. She is one of those girls who need never make

17. *The Apprentice Fiction of F. Scott Fitzgerald*, pp. 91–92.
18. *Smart Set* text, p. 87.

the slightest effort to have men fall in love with them.
Two types of men seldom do: dull men are usually
afraid of her cleverness and intellectual men are usually afraid of her beauty. All others are hers by natural
prerogative.

If ROSALIND could be spoiled the process would have been
complete by this time, and as a matter of fact, her disposition is not all it should be; she wants what she wants
when she wants it and she is prone to make every one
around her pretty miserable when she doesn't get it—
but in the true sense she is not spoiled. Her fresh enthusiasm, her will to grow and learn, her endless faith
in the inexhaustibility of romance, her courage and fundamental honesty—these things are not spoiled.

There are long periods when she cordially loathes her
whole family. She is quite unprincipled; her philosophy
is carpe diem for herself and laissez faire for others. She
loves shocking stories: she has that coarse streak that
usually goes with natures that are both fine and big.
She wants people to like her, but if they do not it never
worries her or changes her.

She is by no means a model character.

The education of all beautiful women is the knowledge of
men. ROSALIND had been disappointed in man after
man as individuals, but she had great faith in man as a
sex. Women she detested. They represented qualities
that she felt and despised in herself—incipient meanness, conceit, cowardice, and petty dishonesty. She once
told a roomful of her mother's friends that the only excuse for women was the necessity for a disturbing element among men. She danced exceptionally well, drew
cleverly but hastily, and had a startling facility with
words, which she used only in love-letters.

But all criticism of ROSALIND ends in her beauty. There was that shade of glorious yellow hair, the desire to imitate which supports the dye industry. There was the eternal kissable mouth, small, slightly sensual, and utterly disturbing. There were gray eyes and an unimpeachable skin with two spots of vanishing color. She was slender and athletic, without underdevelopment, and it was a delight to watch her move about a room, walk along a street, swing a golf club, or turn a "cartwheel."

A last qualification—her vivid, instant personality escaped that conscious, theatrical quality that AMORY had found in ISABELLE. MONSIGNOR DARCY would have been quite up a tree whether to call her a personality or a personage. She was perhaps the delicious, inexpressible, once-in-a-century blend. [Pp. 182–84.]

In the *Nassau Lit* and the *Smart Set*, "The Débutante" had been a light, humorous play with no real conclusion. Fitzgerald had simply provided a stage for one of the heroines who would later make him famous. In the new manuscript, however, he had transformed the material into the emotional high point of his book. For the middle and the end, he had drawn freely on his own recent experiences with Zelda and had forced himself to deal with her rejection of him. Her motives, like Rosalind's, were sensible but cold. As Fitzgerald saw it, she had chosen material security and social acceptance over love. This pattern later became an important part of his outlook on relationships between men and women. Men were romantics, women were pragmatists. The distinction, almost an obsession with him in later years, is found in much of his mature fiction—in short stories like "'The Sensible Thing'" and "Winter Dreams," and of course in *The Great Gatsby*.

In chapter 2, "Experiments in Convalescence," Fitzgerald again drew on recent personal experience. When he had returned to New York in June 1919 after Zelda had broken off with him, he had gone on a long drinking spree, the first serious bender of his life. The experience was still fresh, but even this early in his career he was able to objectify his recent behavior and create excellent fiction from it. The account of Amory's spree in the novel is effective. The third-person narrator recognizes that Amory's behavior, though based on genuine grief, is partly posed and calculated for effect. This acute insight shows Fitzgerald at his perceptive best.

Fitzgerald worked hard on chapter 2. It is the first chapter in the novel done entirely from new material and is also the first chapter since book 1, chapter 1, that is holograph draft throughout. Fitzgerald's handwriting here reveals his method. His script is much smaller than usual; letters and words are carefully inscribed; revisions are few and precise. Such evidence identifies the draft as a fair copy of an earlier version. Fitzgerald was taking pains to get his new material into shape. Organization was still a problem: "Experiments in Convalescence" breaks into two sections—Amory's spree in June 1919 and his literary conversations later that summer with Tom D'Invilliers—but because Fitzgerald composed carefully, putting his material through at least two drafts, the chapter is successful.

Unfortunately Fitzgerald was not nearly so careful with chapter 3, "Young Irony." In fact his carelessness here almost wrecks the development of Amory's character in the second half of the novel. The history of "Young Irony" is complex. It was part of *The Romantic Egotist;* an early version is preserved in the Donahoe typescripts. Sample collations between this early typescript and the carbon typescript that Fitzgerald revised and salvaged for *This Side of Paradise* show that at least one version intervened between the two, but that version does not survive. The typescript that Fitzgerald inserted into the manuscript is a later short-story version of the material. He worked it up in New York during the spring of 1919 and sent it to *Scribner's Magazine*, which turned it down on 18 June. Fitzgerald kept this rejected typescript and made it part of his novel.

The physical characteristics of this typescript play an important part in Fitzgerald's revision of the chapter. The document is single-spaced with very narrow margins, and the typing is crammed on the pages, with almost no room for revision. In several spots Fitzgerald actually had to erase old revisions in order to make new ones. He should have written out a fresh draft in longhand, but he was nearing the end of his novel and was in a hurry. As a result he did little major revising. Certainly he did not think about this material and plan a strategy of incorporation as he had done with "The Débutante." In fact most of his revisions simply change first-person narration to third-person narration. The other passages are allowed to stand with no significant alterations.

This skimpy revising caused some blunders. For instance, on page 241 of the first edition, Eleanor, perched atop a haystack in a thunderstorm, says to Amory, "I know who you are—you're the blond boy that likes 'Ulalume'—I recognize your voice." But Amory has auburn hair. In fact on the very next page Eleanor tells him that she will not call him Don Juan "because you've got reddish hair." As it turns out, the blond hair on page 241 belongs to Stephen Palms. The typescript that Fitzgerald was salvaging had the blond Stephen as hero. In his haste Fitzgerald failed to change Stephen's blond hair to Amory's auburn hair, and the error made it into print. The mistake can be found in every edition of *This Side of Paradise* ever published.

The hair-color business is noticeable but not serious—it merely shows Fitzgerald's haste. More damaging is the fact that the short-story typescript has a college undergraduate for a protagonist. Deleted passages show that Stephen was visiting Eleanor the summer before his senior year at Princeton. Fitzgerald was so determined to use the "Young Irony" material that he lifted it out of Stephen's prewar life and dropped it, largely unchanged, among Amory's postwar experiences. The decision to use this particular material was sound: properly reworked and incorporated, as "The Débutante" had been, "Young Irony" could have been a very good chapter. Eleanor—materialistic, atheistic, and deeply disturbed—has a bad effect on Amory, who has already been disillusioned about women by Rosalind. But Fitzgerald did not revise Stephen's callow undergraduate behavior out of the typescript, and Amory's immature, adolescent posturings in the novel therefore seem odd. He is supposedly a twenty-three-year-old graduate of a sophisticated eastern university and a combat veteran of World War I, but he moons over Eleanor, spouts clichés and bad epigrams, and composes mediocre poetry at the dinner table. Obviously this is not really Amory. It is young Stephen Palms, a rising senior at Princeton, transmogrified into yet another version of Amory Blaine. "Young Irony" is the weakest chapter in book 2; it damages the novel and introduces new inconsistencies into Amory's personality. The Amory of book 2 is a coherent, well-developed character if one ignores the "Young Irony" chapter; but no reader can do this, and Amory's character becomes even more confused.

Chapter 4, "The Supercilious Sacrifice," is fresh material. The chapter, holograph draft throughout, contains little interesting evidence for discussion. There are no revised typescript sheets, no inserted passages, nothing notable about Fitzgerald's handwriting or revisions. The chapter was composed as one unit, designed to fit into the novel just as it does. This fact is noteworthy, especially when one thinks of the disorganized chapters that Fitzgerald had hashed together for *The Romantic Egotist* two years earlier. By the summer of 1919 he had learned—apparently on his own—to block out a chapter, think it through, and write it as a functional unit of a novel.

In "The Supercilious Sacrifice" he works toward a conclusion for his book. Amory, once confident and hopeful, now seems listless and dispirited. In the shoddy episode in Atlantic City with Alec Connage and his gaudy blonde, however, Amory finally learns to do "the next thing," as Monsignor Darcy has urged him to do. What "the next thing" will be in future months Amory does not know, but he at least learns that he cannot idle and dream his life away. At the end of the chapter he is stripped of his ties with the past. He loses Rosalind to the wealthy Dawson Ryder, loses his small income to bankruptcy, and loses Monsignor Darcy to death. Amory has broken with the past.[19]

In the final chapter of the book, "The Egotist Becomes a Personage," Fitzgerald was again working with fresh material and composing in longhand. Only one item is salvaged from previous writing: the opening sixteen lines of verse, untitled in the novel, are a poem called "The Way of Purgation." The brief lyric was Fitzgerald's first commercial sale; *Poet Lore* had bought it almost two years before but had never published it, and Fitzgerald therefore used it as an epigraph.[20] The rest of the chapter is new writing, and excellent writing. The opening prose sequence is the best piece of lengthy description

19. "The Supercilious Sacrifice" was based in part on a 1918 episode in which Fitzgerald, on leave from Camp Mills, was apprehended by a house detective in the Hotel Astor with a naked girl. See Bruccoli, *Epic Grandeur*, p. 93.

20. An undated letter from Fitzgerald to Edmund Wilson, *Letters*, pp. 319–21, identifies the untitled poem as "The Way of Purgation."

in the novel. Amory stands under a theatre porte-cochère, watches New York respond to a sudden shower, and then boards a bus where he sits exploring his mind in an interior dialogue. Fitzgerald took meticulous pains with this section. The handwriting is abnormally small; revisions are precise and clearly lettered. Again, this is a fair copy made from an earlier draft or drafts.

This chapter also contains Amory's meeting with the Big Man and the Little Man, a confrontation in which he argues in favor of socialism. This sequence reveals much about Amory. He is walking to Princeton, making a pilgrimage to say farewell to his past, and is given a ride by the Big Man. This Big Man, a wealthy industrialist riding in a chauffeur-driven limousine, is accompanied by the Little Man, an assistant or clerk. Amory and the Little Man talk, and soon Amory finds himself, to his surprise, arguing vehemently for socialism. He has never been radical; his politics in college were nonexistent. But socialism in 1919 was in the air; the recent Russian Revolution was looked upon as a great political experiment, and many young intellectuals—among them Fitzgerald's friend Edmund Wilson—were leaning toward socialism. Fitzgerald is showing in this chapter how an educated, talented, articulate young man might be driven by economic and social inequities in America to take up socialism. Amory is ripe for conversion: he is "sick of a system where the richest man gets the most beautiful girl if he wants her, where the artist without an income has to sell his talents to a button manufacturer" (p. 299).

But Amory's glib arguments do not reveal profound changes in "the fundamental Amory." Fitzgerald makes it clear that Amory has not been won over by the socialists. For one thing, Amory's sudden conversion is a personal thing based entirely on self-interest. Asked by the Big Man if he is "one of these parlor Bolsheviks, one of these idealists," Amory replies, "If being an idealist is both safe and lucrative, I might try it" (pp. 289–90). The most obvious irony is that Amory, as a socialist, should pity the lower classes, but he has only contempt for them. He says to the Big Man, "The lower classes are narrower, less pleasant and personally more selfish—certainly more stupid" (p. 291). His aristocratic background and Princeton education are still powerful influences on him. He does not want to be a socialist; he wants to be a "big man," but he wonders if someone with his particular talents can ever reach that goal in America.

The manuscript here is clearly first draft from beginning to end and is remarkably free of revisions and cuts. Fitzgerald composed the Big Man/Little Man section briskly and confidently. As he approached the end of his novel, however, he faced a dilemma. He had instructions from Scribner's to give his book a definite ending. The rejection letter had been insistent on that point: "The story does not seem to us to work up to a conclusion," Scribner's had written. "Neither the hero's career nor his character are shown to be brought to any stage which justifies an ending." Scribner's had been blunt: "It seems to us in short that the story does not culminate in anything." The message was obvious. If Fitzgerald wanted Scribner's to publish his novel, he would have to provide a proper conclusion for it. But how could he do so? Amory has finished with adolescence and is about to enter manhood, but he still has no clear direction for his life. His major accomplishment has been to learn about his own personality, and his real life is only now beginning. How, then, can his story "culminate in anything"?

Fitzgerald hit on a brilliant solution. In the final line of the manuscript he left Amory poised on the edge of manhood, finished with his education but unsure of his future. Amory stands beneath the stars, stretches out his arms to the "crystalline, radiant sky," and delivers his final line. In the published book it reads:

"I know myself," he cried, "but that is all."

In the manuscript, however, there is no final period. Instead the sentence ends with a *dash*. Under pressure, Fitzgerald had again come up with a startling insight. The significance of that final dash is readily apparent. During the novel Amory has adopted, one after another, various creeds and philosophies, always in search of a system that will explain reality to him. All these systems—Catholicism, the Princeton social system, American-Dream capitalism, and socialism—have failed him, and by the end of the book he is bitterly disillusioned. He has learned that no system can make sense out of the world he has seen and experienced. Amory has found no answers, but in his quest he has at least learned to know himself. The dash therefore echoes back through the entire novel and gives a modest, hesitant tone to Amory's final line. With the dash Amory says that he knows little, but that he does know himself. He also knows that whatever he accomplishes in life will depend on how well he can control his own erratic imagination and troublesome personality. Amory is not confident about his future; his most important struggles lie ahead of him. The dash leaves the novel open-ended and makes Amory's final statement a preface to his future, not a summation of his past.

The dash also explains the third and final title of the novel— *This Side of Paradise*. Just as *The Romantic Egotist* had become "The Romantic Egotist," the title of book 1, so now his working title, *The Education of a Personage*, became "The Education of a Personage," the title of book 2. Amory's education is complete; he has gained self-awareness and has become a "personage." This process has left him, in Rupert

Brooke's phrase, "this side of paradise." The dash dovetails with the new title. Amory—who knows himself, but that is all—is now "this side of paradise," about to begin his adult life.

But this dash, crucial to the meaning of the novel, was changed to a period before the book got into print. And the period in the published text gives a different tone to the ending by making Amory's statement a definite, arrogant pronouncement. Self-knowledge is no longer preliminary; it is instead an end in itself. A good example of the sort of criticism generated by this final period is found in John McCormick's study *The Middle Distance: A Comparative History of American Imaginative Literature: 1919–1932* (New York: Free Press, 1971). McCormick writes:

Because he was a moralist, Fitzgerald wrote novels of ideas of a sort. Part of his power as a writer derived from his incapacity for abstract thought. Lacking intellectual tidiness, he was forced to grope his way through narrative, through the fictional comings and goings of his characters, to an essence which he himself grasped imperfectly and fleetingly. In *This Side of Paradise*, that subterranean idea has to do with the adolescent's necessity for pose, for role-playing in order to arm himself against the onslaughts of an uncomprehending world. The closest Fitzgerald came to expressing his idea occurs at the conclusion, when Amory Blaine, shorn of illusion and finished with poses, "stretched out his arms to the crystalline, radiant sky. 'I know myself,' he cried, 'but that is all'." The gesture, reminiscent of D. H. Lawrence's conclusion to *Sons and Lovers* and of many novels of the period, takes the place of thought and sets a grandiloquent full stop to the novel. It is conventional in a novel that was received as unconventional, familiar to the point of cliché. [P. 320.]

Who changed the dash to a period, and why? Unfortunately, the extant documentary evidence is inconclusive. Fitzgerald may have made the change; Perkins may have made it; or a typist, copy editor, compositor, or proofreader may have done it. And if Fitzgerald did make the change, he may have been under pressure from Perkins or Scribner's to do so.

The only extant prepublication form of the novel is the manuscript. No ribbon typescript, carbon typescript, galley or page proofs survive. The change from dash to period could have been made in any intermediate form of typescript or proof, and it could have been made by anyone who had a hand in the composition, typing, editing, typesetting, or proofing of the novel. Two important pieces of tangential evidence survive: the letter from Scribner's rejecting *The Romantic Egotist* and a preface Fitzgerald wrote for *This Side of Paradise* but did not publish with it. The letter reveals the attitude of Scribner's, and probably of Maxwell Perkins, toward *The Romantic Egotist*. Scribner's wanted a definite ending, and as a beginner, Fitzgerald would have paid close attention to the wishes of his prospective publisher. The preface, unpublished during Fitzgerald's lifetime, is also important:

> Two years ago, when I was a very young man indeed, I had an unmistakable urge to write a book. It was to be a picaresque novel, original in form and alternating a melancholy, naturalistic egotism with a picture of the generation then hastening to war.
>
> It was to be naive in places, shocking in others, painful to the conventional and not without its touch of ironic sublimity. The "leading character", a loiterer on the borderland of genius, loved many women and gazed at himself in many mirrors—in fact, women and mirrors were preponderant in all the important scenes.

I completed it during the last gasp of a last year at college, and the intricacies of a training camp. Its epigrams
were polished by the substitution of the word *one* for the
word *you;* its chapter titles were phrased to sound somewhat like lines from pre-Raphaelite poems, somewhat like
electric signs over musical comedies; the book itself was a
tedius casserole of a dozen by McKenzie, Wells, and Robert Hugh Benson, largely flavored by the great undigested
butterball of *Dorian Gray.*

The conservative publisher to whom I sent it kept it for
several months and finally returned it with the complaint
that the hero failed in the end to find himself, and that this
defection would so certainly disappoint the reader as to
predestine the book to failure.

He suggested that I remedy this and I pondered the difficulty for several weeks—how I could intrigue the hero
into a "philosphy of life" when my own ideas were in
much the state of Alice's after the hatter's tea-party.

At length I took a tip from Schopenhauer, Hugh Wal-
pole, and even the early Wells—begged the question by
plunging boldly into obscurity; astounded myself with an
impenetrable chapter where I left the hero alone with
rhapsodic winds and hyper-significant stars: gemmed the
paragrpahs with neo-symbolic bits culled from my own
dismantled poems—such awe-inspiring half lines as * * *
the dark celibacy of greatness * * * Youth, the Queen Anne
Clavichord from which age wrings the symphony of art
* * * the tired pitying beauty of monotony that hung like
summer air over the gate of his soul * * *

And finding that I had merely dragged the hero from a
logical muddle into an illogical one, I dispatched him to
the war and callously slew him several thousand feet in
the air, whence he fell "not like a dead but a splendid life-

found swallow **** down **** down ****"

The book finished with four dots—there was a fifth but I erased it.

After two months it was again refused. The conservative publisher was, however, optimistic enough to send it to a more radical competitor, who specialized in leading out the new Slavic novelists and giving free air to experiments in Celtic phrasing. This publisher did not even faintly consider it.

The war over, I slumped into a mental lethargy in the misty depths of which I searched for the causes of my book's failure, and eventually discovered the root of the trouble. All I had written of things I was interested in: THE INFLUENCE OF NIGHT, RATHER BAD WOMEN, PERSONALITY, FANATICISM, THE SUPERNATURAL, and VERY GOOD WOMEN was quite above the average.

All I had written of subjects with which I was thoroughly cognizant: THE "PREP" SCHOOL, COLLEGE, THE MIDDLE WEST, NATURE, QUAINT STUPID PEOPLE, and MYSELF was, because I was quite bored with all of them, well below average.

My course was obvious, my inspiration was immediate. Virtuously resisting the modern writer's tendency to dramatize himself, I began another novel; whether its hero really "gets anywhere" is for the reader to decide.

For bait to the hesitant I hold out the promise that the words *passion, moonlight, era* and *God* occur many times; the words *shimee, debutante* and *mystic* with less frequency.

Resisting a temptation to dedicate it either to a certain prelate—who would quite possibly be exhumed and excommunicated—or, throwing guile aside, to "myself, with love and affection," I offer it to all those argumentative and discoursive souls who once frequented a certain inn whose doors are now dark, whose fabled walls ring no more to the melody of Chaucer's lesser known poems.

> F. Scott Fitzgerald
> St. Paul, Minn.
> Mid-August, 1919[21]

In this preface Fitzgerald is still preoccupied with, and unsure about, the ending of his book. And there is the puzzling business about the five dots, one of which was later erased. Was Fitzgerald referring to the dash in his manuscript? Perhaps, but he was writing about the revised version of *The Romantic Egotist*, not about *This Side of Paradise*, and he was talking about dots, not a dash.

A typist, copy editor, compositor, or proofreader would have had one simple motive for changing the dash—the belief that a novel should not end in a dash, that someone had made a mistake, and that changing the punctuation mark to a period would be a favor to the author. This explanation is possible but not likely. Underlings in publishing houses and printing shops frequently do change punctuation, but it would take a particularly imperceptive person not to recognize the importance of that final dash. Fitzgerald or Perkins would have noticed the alteration, and either man could have restored the dash in proof.

Perkins is a more likely suspect. He had taken a special interest in Fitzgerald and had pushed hard for acceptance of *This Side of Paradise*. He had insisted that Fitzgerald's hero get somewhere, that the novel have a true conclusion. By nature and background Perkins was conservative, and he might

21. Quoted from the facsimile in the *Fitzgerald/Hemingway Annual 1971*, pp. 1–2.

have thought the final dash "gimmicky." And we know from his later handling of Thomas Wolfe that he was not reluctant to make significant editorial changes in authors' manuscripts.

Fitzgerald's possible motives are more complex. He was under pressure to give his novel a definite conclusion. As a young unknown, he did not have leverage enough to insist on his own ending. Perkins might have suggested changing the dash to a period, and Fitzgerald, anxious to please, might have gone along. Or Fitzgerald might have decided on his own that a period was better, less risky, than a dash.

The ending of *This Side of Paradise* is therefore a puzzle. Should it conclude with a dash or a period? The evidence favors the dash, but only slightly. It is there in the manuscript, written in Fitzgerald's hand, whereas the period in the published text might have been put there by any one of several persons. The period carries no definite authorial sanction, and there is a strong possibility that Perkins put it into the book, or insisted that Fitzgerald do so. We know who put the dash in the manuscript: Fitzgerald put it there. Were I to edit a critical edition of *This Side of Paradise*, I would print the dash.[22]

Fitzgerald made mistakes in composing *This Side of Paradise*, errors that a more experienced, fully matured professional would not have made. But much of the appeal of his novel lies in its many surfaces and attitudes, which reflect his own uncertain state of mind while he was writing the book. Point-of-view is irregular and characterization inconsistent, but some-

22. Fate seems to throw these questions in my path. For another famous American novel with two possible endings, see the recent Pennsylvania edition of Theodore Dreiser's *Sister Carrie* (Philadelphia: University of Pennsylvania Press, 1981). As textual editor of this edition I chose to retain Dreiser's earlier ending, the one his initial instinct told him was right. There is no connection in my own mind between my decisions on *Sister Carrie* and *This Side of Paradise*, but the parallels are interesting.

how the entire collection—fragments from this play and that short story, pages from this novel and that typescript, borrowings from this letter and that diary—all of these bits hold together. Rewritten with a uniform point-of-view and a consistent attitude toward Amory, *This Side of Paradise* would have been more polished, but it would undoubtedly have lost much of its charm and liveliness. For all his reuse of old material, Fitzgerald still made a moving story, with engaging characters and incidents, and with an important theme. *This Side of Paradise* breaks many rules, but as a novel it succeeds.

4

Grammarian, Typist, and Editor

Fitzgerald finished the first draft of *The Education of a Personage* on 25 July 1919. The next day he wrote to Maxwell Perkins:

Dear Mr. Perkins:
After four months attempt to write commercial copy by day and painful half-hearted imitations of popular literature by night I decided that it was one thing or another. So I gave up getting married and went home.

Yesterday I finished the first draft of a novel called

THE EDUCATION OF A PERSONAGE

It is in no sense a revision of the ill-fated *Romantic Egotist* but it contains some of the former material improved and worked over and bears a strong family resemblance besides.

But while the other was a tedius, disconnected casserole this is definate attempt at a big novel and I really believe I have hit it, as immediately I stopped disciplining the muse she trotted obediently around and became an erratic mistress if not a steady wife.

Now what I want to ask you is this—if I send you the book by August 20th and you decide you could risk its publication (I am blatantly confident that you will) would it be brought out in October, say, or just what would decide its date of publication?

This is an odd question I realize especially since you havn't even seen the book but you have been so kind in the past about my stuff that I venture to intrude once more upon your patience.[1]

Fitzgerald wanted early publication because he hoped his novel would win Zelda back. With the book in hand he would have evidence of the beginnings of a literary career, an actual profession. But Fitzgerald knew nothing about commercial book production, and Perkins had to write back and explain some details:

July 28, 1919

Dear Mr. Fitzgerald:

Your letter about "The Education of a Personage" (which strikes us as an excellent title) arouses a great curiosity to see the manuscript. But there is one thing certain: no publisher could publish this book in October without greatly injuring its chances; for the canvasing of the trade for the fall season began several months ago, and the book sellers have invested their money in fall books, and would now order grudgingly, and in much lesser quantities than they would at the beginning of a season. Your book for its own advantage ought to be published after January 1st, all the more because you will be a new author and should have every advantage of carefully prepared publicity. The book should be talked up ahead of its appearance to the trade: they should see sheets in advance, etc. This is the plain truth of the matter. The book should be published in February or March, and the selling of it should begin before Christmas.

1. *Dear Scott/Dear Max*, p. 17. Subsequent quotations in this chapter from the Fitzgerald-Perkins correspondence are taken from this edition, pp. 18–27.

But we hope you will let us see this manuscript. Ever since the first reading of your first manuscript we have felt that you would succeed.

Fitzgerald was anxious to submit his novel, but he was also apprehensive about his erratic spelling and grammar. He had cause to worry: his drafts were filled with mechanical errors. After completing the manuscript, he therefore had someone read it and make suggestions for improvement. This reader went through and marked some 188 instances of rough syntax, misspelling, faulty grammar, improper style, and questionable content.

The reader has not been identified. Fitzgerald was in St. Paul, and the reader may have been a friend or former teacher from the area. Beyond this possibility, there is no indication of who he might have been. In this study he will be called "Grammarian" after the figure in Browning's poem "A Grammarian's Funeral." Fitzgerald's Grammarian was not a scholar grinding away at the Greek particles, but he was a conscientious person about the rules and conventions of written language. The borrowed name seems appropriate.

Most of Grammarian's markings are decipherable. He used a hard-lead black pencil, and his touch was lighter than Fitzgerald's. His handwriting, a thin masculine scrawl, is often difficult to read, and is easily distinguished from Fitzgerald's bold, rounded script. Grammarian's method was to mark a reading with a check mark or a question mark in the left-hand margin. Sometimes he added the initials "P.G." for "Poor Grammar." He often underscored or circled the words he wanted Fitzgerald to change. Some of these markings were later erased or deleted, but they are still recoverable. Grammarian's written comments are few and short and are found mostly toward the end of the manuscript. After reading and marking the text so that he could relocate questionable readings, Grammarian apparently went back over the manuscript with Fitzgerald, explained what his marks meant, and made his suggestions. Beside Grammarian's notations Fitzgerald has almost invariably revised the text.

Grammarian's influence was both good and bad. On the positive side, he pointed out many errors in mechanics and word usage. For example, Fitzgerald usually wrote *disallusioned* for *disillusioned*, and Grammarian had him correct these mistakes. He also pointed out Fitzgerald's overuse of the phrase *a sort of* and prompted him to supply better readings. Fitzgerald's *cop* became a *policeman* at Grammarian's suggestion—a change that may show his sense of propriety. Similarly, Fitzgerald had written about chunks of Milton and Shakespeare that Amory's English teachers had been cramming down his throat. Grammarian seems to have felt that such treatment of classic English authors was in poor taste, and beside his check mark Fitzgerald reworded to "what morsels of Shakespeare and Milton had been recently forced upon him" (p. 55).

These spot revisions improved the text. With Grammarian's help, Fitzgerald avoided some obvious blunders and rewrote some poor sentences. But Grammarian did not do a thorough job: he overlooked Fitzgerald's use of *ingenious* for *ingenuous*, for example, and he seems to have despaired of marking the multitudinous misspellings. Grammarian did help, however, by pointing out many demonstrable errors, misused words, and inappropriate readings.

On the negative side, much of Grammarian's advice was picky and schoolmarmish. He was a stickler, for example, about removing prepositions from the ends of sentences. An important thematic statement toward the end of the published novel reads, "What ghosts were people with which to work!"

(p. 301). Fitzgerald could hardly have written such an execrable sentence on his own; he introduced the wording at Grammarian's suggestion, to remove a preposition from the end of the sentence. Similarly, Cecelia Connage, Rosalind's precocious younger sister, complains about having to sit out a dance intermission with her brother Alec. He offers to leave, but she responds, in the original reading, "Good heavens no—who would I begin the next dance with?"[2] Grammarian, alert to the final preposition, checked the line and wrote "P.G." in the margin. In the revised reading, young Cecelia says stiffly, "Good heavens no—with whom would I begin the next dance?" (p. 195). These two changes are typical of many in the manuscript. Grammarian's influence makes some of Fitzgerald's writing, especially his dialogue, sound unnatural and strained.

Even more serious are the cuts that Grammarian recommended. Beside his marginal check marks, an exuberant description of Monsignor Darcy as "all things to all people" was removed. Why Grammarian disliked the passage is not clear since he wrote no marginal comment, but his arguments must have been persuasive since Fitzgerald made the cut. In the excised passage, Fitzgerald had described Monsignor as a favorite of old ladies, old priests, middle-class and aristocratic Catholics. To these people Monsignor was conservative or modern, solid or entertaining, enthusiastic or exemplary, as the situation demanded. Grammarian likely thought the passage unrealistic: no one person can be so versatile. But that is just the point with Monsignor. He is meant to be unrealistic, even fantastic and magical. His chameleon-like behavior in the cut lines matches the rest of his personality exactly. It is unfortunate that Fitzgerald was persuaded to remove the passage.

2. Quoted from the facsimile in *"This Side of Paradise," The Grammarian, and the "Author's Final Intentions"* (Blacksburg, Va., 1972).

Also revised and softened at Grammarian's suggestion was an attack on certain Princeton professors who gathered circles of fawning students about them. Fitzgerald implied that these professors had themselves missed popularity in college and now played up to popular football heroes or other campus idols. In its original form the passage contributes to an important subtheme of *This Side of Paradise*—the ineffectuality of the American educational system. Fitzgerald should probably have left the passage intact.

Grammarian was also something of a prude. In the margins beside a sensual, saccharine kissing scene between Amory and Rosalind, he wrote "Bromides!" Fitzgerald obligingly toned down the passage. But the Rosalind-Amory affair should be overly sentimental. That is what Rosalind has wanted from her men but has failed to get. She tells Amory on the night they fall in love, "I want sentiment, real sentiment—and I never find it" (p. 198). But she does find deep emotional involvement with Amory, and she uses him for it. The dialogue in this early love scene was mindless and sentimental because it was supposed to be.

Finally, when Amory first meets Eleanor Savage she tells him (in the unrevised version) that if he will not speak until they walk to the crossroads, she will kiss him good night. She makes her promise good, and as Amory feels her warm lips on his, "a deep singing came out of the fields and filled his way homeward" (pp. 246–47). Grammarian objected to the casual impropriety of the kiss. He penciled a check mark and "Why?" in the margin, and both Eleanor's promise and her kiss came out. In the revised reading the fields still sing to Amory, but the reader has no idea why they do. Eleanor is unconventional and daring, and she loves to shock people; she is the most sexually liberated girl in the novel. Giving a good-night kiss to a strange but handsome boy is quite in character for her.

Grammarian's "Why?" simply shows that he had never met, as
Fitzgerald had, a girl like Eleanor.

Fitzgerald took Grammarian's advice readily: of the 188
marked readings, 169 were revised. Some revisions are minor,
others are more extensive. Some are improvements, but others
are indifferent, and still others are harmful. Grammar has
been altered—sometimes for the better, sometimes needlessly.
Dialogue has been "primped up," destroying natural rhythms
and idioms and introducing stiff diction. Characterization has
been altered: Monsignor Darcy is more realistic; Rosalind and
Amory are not as affectionate; Eleanor is less daring. Grammarian had a significant influence on the text of the novel.

After satisfying Grammarian, Fitzgerald was finished with the
manuscript. The next step was to get the novel in shape for
submission to Scribner's. In mid-August Perkins wrote, asking
to see sample chapters, and Fitzgerald responded with a long,
informative letter:

August 16th, 1919

Dear Mr. Perkins:

I appreciated both your letters and I'm sure you wont be
dissapointed in the book when you get it. It is a well-
considered, finished *whole* this time and I think its a more
crowded (in the best sense) piece of work than has been
published in this country for some years.

It is finished, except for one last revision or rather correction and the typewriting, so I think you'll get it before
September 1st. As to sample chapters—it seems hardly
worth while to send them to you now. The title has been
changed to

This Side of Paradise

from those lines of Rupert Brookes
. . . Well, this side of paradise
There's little comfort in the wise.

About two chapters are from my old book, completely
changed and rewritten, the rest is new material.
On the next page I've written the chapter names.

BOOK I
The Romantic Egotist

Chapter I   Amory, son of Beatrice
"   II   Spires and Gargoyles
"   III   The Egotist considers

Interlude
March 1917—February 1919

BOOK II
The Education of a Personage

Chapter I   The Debutante
"   II   Experiments in Convalescense
"   III   Young Irony
"   IV   The Supercillious Sacrifice
"   V   The Egotist becomes a Personage

Book One   contains about 35,000 words
The Interlude   "   "   4,000 words
Book Two   "   "   47,000 words
Total   "   "   86,000 words

About publication—I asked you the chances of an early
publication (in case you take it) for two reasons: first—
because I want to get started both in a literary and financial way; second—because it is to some extent a timely

book and it seems to me that the public are wild for decent reading matter—"Dangerous Days" and "Ramsey Milholland"—My God!

Fitzgerald did not know how to type, so he turned his manuscript over to someone who did. Because no ribbon typescript of *This Side of Paradise* survives it is impossible to know what changes the typist made in the text or what alterations Fitzgerald made when he got the typescript back. A collation of the manuscript with the first printing, however, suggests some things about the typing job. Unfortunately it was not especially good. The typist was careless about underlinings: numerous words underscored for emphasis in the manuscript are not in italics in the published text.[3] Fitzgerald used italics carefully, sometimes underlining only one syllable of a word to suggest exaggerated pronunciation. Amory, for example, should pronounce the word *fright*fully when he tries to impress Myra St. Claire's mother, not *frightfully* as he does in the published book, but the typist must have missed the distinction and underscored the whole word. The typist also had a bad habit of typing readings that Fitzgerald had crossed through.[4] There were misreadings—a word that should have been typed as *sewed* became *served* and the word *unimpeachable* became *an impeachable*. The word *plainly* became *faintly*, *muster* became *master*, and *listlessly* became *blissfully*. And there were misunderstood directions. In the biggest blunder, the typist failed to follow directions penciled in the margin and caused a major confusion of sentences and para-

3. These include "was" at 3.18 of the first edition, "atmosphere" at 4.29, "American Society" at 29.6, "preparatory" at 29.33, and "vulnerable" at 148.24.

4. For instance, "plainly" at 11.13 of the first edition and "this voice" at 265.19 are both deleted readings in the manuscript.

graphs. The facsimile below shows how the text of the section should be arranged.

No real purpose is served by criticizing an anonymous typist. Fitzgerald's manuscript was messy and confusing, and he should have caught these typing errors himself before sending his novel off. But when possible, the accuracy of any non-authorial hand that worked with the text should be assessed.

Fitzgerald sent the typescript of *This Side of Paradise* to Scribner's on 4 September 1919. He wanted the novel to arrive with a flourish; so he asked his friend Thomas Daniels, who happened to be traveling to New York, to hand-deliver the typescript to the Scribner offices. After Daniels had left, Fitzgerald wrote Perkins:

> *Sept. 4th 1919.*
>
> *Dear Mr. Perkins:*
> I sent the book today under a separate cover. I want to discuss a few things in connection with it.
>
> You'll notice that it contains much material from the *Romantic Egotist.*
>
> (1) Chapter II Bk I of the present book contains material from "Spires & Gargoyles, Ha-Ha-Hortense, Babes in the Wood & Crecendo"—rewritten in third person, cut down and re-edited
>
> (2) Chapter III Bk I contains material from "Second descent of the Egotist and the Devil." rewritten ect.
>
> (3) Chapter IV Bk I contains material from "The Two Mystics, Clara & the End of Many Things"
>
> (4) Chapter III Bk II is a revision of Eleanor in 3d person—with that fur incident left out.
>
> Chapter I Bk I, & Chaps I, II, IV, & V of Bk II are entirely new.

fact, her disposition is not all it should be; she wants what she wants when she wants it and she is prone to make every one around her pretty miserable when she doesn't get it—but in the true sense she is not spoiled. Her fresh enthusiasm, her will to grow and learn, her endless faith in the inexhaustibility of romance, her courage and fundamental honesty—these things are not spoiled.

There are long periods when she cordially loathes her whole family. She is quite unprincipled; her philosophy is carpe diem for herself and laissez faire for others. She loves shocking stories: she has that coarse streak that usually goes with natures that are both fine and big. She wants people to like her, but if they do not it never worries her or changes her.

She is by no means a model character.

The education of all beautiful women is the knowledge of men. ROSALIND *had been disappointed in man after man as individuals, but she had great faith in man as a sex. Women she detested. They represented qualities that she felt and despised in herself—incipient meanness, conceit, cowardice, and petty dishonesty. She once told a roomful of her mother's friends that the only excuse for women was the necessity for a disturbing element among men. She danced exceptionally well, drew cleverly but hastily, and had a startling facility with words, which she used only in love-letters.*

But all criticism of ROSALIND *ends in her beauty. There was that shade of glorious yellow hair, the desire to imitate which supports the dye industry. There was the eternal kissable mouth, small, slightly sensual, and utterly disturbing. There*

Page 183 from the first printing of *This Side of Paradise*, marked to show the proper order of the text. The sentence beginning "*She is by no means*" should precede the sentence beginning "*There are long periods.*" The resulting paragraph should then be moved to follow the paragraph beginning "*The education of all beautiful women.*"

You'll see that of the old material there is all new use, outside the revision in the 3d person. For instance the Princeton characters of the R.E.—Tom, Tump, Lorry, Lumpy, Fred, Dick, Jim, Burne, Judy, Mcintyre and Jesse have become in this book—Fred, Dick, Alec, Tom, Kerry & Burne. Isabelle & Rosalind of the R.E. have become just Isabelle while the new Rosalind is a different person.

Beatrice is a new character—Dr. Dudly becomes Monsignor Darcy; is much better done—in fact every character is in better perspective.

The preface I leave to your discretion—perhaps its a little too clever-clever; likewise you may object to the literary personalities in Chap II & Bk II and to the length of the socialistic discussion in the last chapter. The book contains a little over ninety thousand words. I certainly think the hero gets somewhere.

I await anxiously your verdict.

The typescript of *This Side of Paradise* presumably reached Scribner's in early September, and this time the decision was prompt. On 16 September 1919 Perkins mailed this letter to Fitzgerald:

Dear Mr. Fitzgerald:

I am very glad, personally, to be able to write to you that we are all for publishing your book, "This Side of Paradise". Viewing it as the same book that was here before, which in a sense it is, though translated into somewhat different terms and extended further, I think that you have improved it enormously. As the first manuscript did, it abounds in energy and life and it seems to me to be in much better proportion. I was afraid that, when we declined the first manuscript, you might be done with us

conservatives. I am glad you are not. The book is so different that it is hard to prophesy how it will sell but we are
all for taking a chance and supporting it with vigor. As for
terms, we shall be glad to pay a royalty of 10% on the first
five thousand copies and of 15% thereafter,—which by the
way, means more than it use to, now that retail prices
upon which the percentage is calculated, have so much
advanced.

Fitzgerald was ecstatic. He wrote back to Perkins on 18
September:

Of course I was delighted to get your letter and I've been
in a sort of trance all day; not that I doubted you'd take it
but at last I have something to show people. It has enough
advertisement in St. Paul already to sell several thousand
copies & I think Princeton will buy it (I've been a periodi-
cal, local Great-Expectations for some time in both places.)

Perkins sent the contract for *This Side of Paradise* to Fitzgerald on 24 September; Fitzgerald signed it and sent it back
three days later. The terms were identical to those in the acceptance letter. Now there was little for Fitzgerald to do but
wait for proofs.

The acceptance of *This Side of Paradise* brought a happy
resolution for Fitzgerald's romance with Zelda. He visited her
in November and, backed by the acceptance of his book, re-
kindled their affair and renewed their engagement. *This Side
of Paradise* was the key. As Zelda wrote to him later, "I am very
proud of you—I hate to say this, but I don't *think* I had much
confidence in you at first. . . . It's so nice to know that you
really *can* do things—*anything*. . . ."[5] Fitzgerald would marry

5. Quoted from Milford, *Zelda*, p. 57.

Zelda on 3 April 1920, just eight days after publication of *This Side of Paradise*. He wanted the two events, representing success and love, to coincide as nearly as possible.

Meanwhile Perkins had the typescript. He had a personal stake in *This Side of Paradise;* he had pushed hard for acceptance of the book, and naturally he wanted to edit it himself. But Perkins, so good at handling authors, was not the man to copy-edit what must have been a mistake-filled typescript. Roger Burlingame, in the Scribner house history, recalls that "the difficulty with *This Side of Paradise* was that Maxwell Perkins would never, at any stage of its making, let it go out of his hands, and Perkins, but for the stern supervision of his secretary, Miss Wyckoff, would probably be something of an orthographic phenomenon himself."[6]

It is difficult to know exactly what Perkins did to the typescript because that document does not survive.[7] Some of the changes between manuscript and first print, however, are almost surely his work. For example, shortly after Amory moves to Minneapolis he writes a note to Myra St. Claire accepting her invitation to a bobbing party. Amory fancies himself a young sophisticate, and he wants to make his billet-doux entirely proper. He is uncertain about how to punctuate the first line of the note, however. After "*My dear Miss St. Claire*" he therefore puts a comma, then adds a colon to be safe, and finally tacks on a dash for good measure. Perkins apparently missed this small touch of humor and regularized the punctuation; in the published book only the colon remains. Perkins may also have been responsible for correcting some of Fitz-

6. Burlingame, *Of Making Many Books*, p. 112.

7. The Bruccoli collection contains forty-eight pages from the carbon typescript of *This Side of Paradise;* these pages comprise chapter 1 and a part of chapter 2 and were sent by Fitzgerald to Stephan Parrott. According to Bruccoli, "Every page was revised before book publication, but the alterations are not major" (*Epic Grandeur*, p. 113n).

gerald's slang spellings; the word *keed*, for instance, becomes just *kid* between manuscript and first print. And a rather good pun apparently perished under the blue pencil. Fitzgerald had used the term *sotto voice* to describe the loud, slurred, "sot-voiced" speech of the drunken Fred Sloane in chapter 3. In the published book, the term has been "fixed" to read *sotto voce*, which translates "in a very soft voice"—not at all what Fitzgerald meant. Perkins may or may not have been responsible for these alterations, but if he was the person who copy-edited the typescript, he probably made the changes.

It is difficult to discover precisely what Perkins did to the typescript, but easy to see what he did not do. He did not check routine spelling and punctuation, and he did not correct a great many grammatical errors. More seriously, he did not verify the spellings of authors' names or the titles of books and poems, nor did he check for accuracy the names of various politicians, movie stars, and sports figures. Of course Fitzgerald was capable of checking these details himself—in fact, he should have done so before sending the book to Scribner's—but he seems to have assumed from the beginning that the publisher would take care of such things. Perkins, however, had not yet edited many books for publication. He had spent his first several years with Scribner's in the advertising department, and he may honestly not have realized what his editorial responsibilities were. He disliked the detailed work of copy-editing and proofreading, and he usually avoided these chores or did them quickly. Besides, Fitzgerald was an alumnus of Princeton, where he had majored in English and had written for the literary magazine. In the novel he had rattled off the names of authors and literary works with the facility of a bookstore clerk; surely he had also spelled these names correctly—or so Perkins must have assumed. As it turned out, no one checked the text for accuracy. Fitzgerald and Perkins each assumed that the other had done so, and the result was a published book peppered with errors.

Both men did see proofs in January and February 1920, but most of their correspondence concerns the physical appearance of the book. Fitzgerald did not like the typography of the subchapter headings, but otherwise he thought the galleys looked "damn good." He did some minor revising in proof—he added H. L. Mencken's name on p. 224, and he substituted Conrad's *Almayer's Folly* for Wells's *The Research Magnificent* on p. 284, for example—but he made no truly major revisions. He had not yet come to treat proof as an opportunity for major revision, as he would do with *The Great Gatsby* and *Tender Is the Night*. Other letters between Perkins and Fitzgerald during these months concern the publication date, dust-jacket artwork, and illustrations (which they decided against). Nowhere is the correctness of the text mentioned.

It does not matter now whose fault the errors were. *This Side of Paradise* is part of literary history, as are the lives and careers of Fitzgerald and Perkins. But these errors would have a significant effect on Fitzgerald's career and reputation, and it is important to trace their origin. In this case, neither the author nor the editor did an accurate job. The first edition of the novel, published late in March, was filled with mistakes, and the reviewers had a field day. The stamp of ignorance and pseudo-intellectuality that this text put on Fitzgerald would taint his career and dog him for the rest of his life.

5

This Side of Paradise

The postpublication history of *This Side of Paradise* is as interesting and instructive as the story of the novel's composition. *This Side of Paradise* is an authentic case in which a bad text significantly affected a book's initial reception and an author's subsequent reputation. The textual history of *This Side of Paradise* is lamentable, but it is not without its moments of perverse humor. Remember the word juvenilia, or juvenalia if you prefer.

The first impression of *This Side of Paradise*, riddled with mistakes, was officially published on 26 March 1920. Fitzgerald soon learned to his considerable embarrassment what kind of condition his text was in. Over the next four months he attempted to patch up the text by sending Perkins several lists of corrections and alterations, and Perkins in turn tried to have these changes made in the plates of *This Side of Paradise*. But neither Fitzgerald nor Perkins was especially good at this kind of detailed work, and they were less than successful. Their correspondence, in fact, is a comedy of errors. The intentions of both men were good, but the results were not.[1]

On 1 April 1920, six days after *This Side of Paradise* was published, Robert Bridges, then editor of *Scribner's Magazine*, typed up an office memo which listed eleven errors:

1. In this chapter, Bridges's list of errors, Fitzgerald's lists of changes, and the letters between Fitzgerald and Perkins are quoted from "The Corrections Lists for F. Scott Fitzgerald's *This Side of Paradise*," *Studies in Bibliography* 26 (1973): 254–64.

THURSDAYm, APRIL 1st, 1920.

E R R O R S   I N   :

"THIS SIDE OF PARADISE".
by
F. SCOTT FITZGERALD

Page 28:　Line 10:"Ex-Ambassador" should be "Ex-Minister."

Page 80:　Line 7 from bottom: "Cambell" Hall should be "Campbell" Hall

Page 128:　Line 13: "Dachari" should be "Daiquiri"

Page 226:　Line 2 from bottom: "Benêt" should be "Benét"

Page 228:	"I restless"	should be	"I am restless" (?)
Page 229:	"Kerenski"	should be	"Kerensky"
Page 229:	"Gunmeyer"	should be	"Guynemer"
Page 232:	"Gouveneer"	should be	Gouverneur"
Page 294:	"Mackeys"	should be	"Mackays".
Page 304, Line 19:	"God's"	should be	"Gods" (plural

I also think the Dedication is wrong and that "Sigorney" should be spelled "Sigourney"; but I can't prove it.

Robert Bridges.

Fitzgerald was in New York City to marry Zelda, and he submitted his own list of mistakes and revisions. On the backs of four sheets of stationery from the Biltmore Hotel—Fitzgerald and Zelda were honeymooning there—he wrote down these changes and sent them to Perkins:

On Dedication page
    Substitute
       Sigourney for *Sigorney*

On page 6, line 7.
change *raconteur* to
the fem. gender

On page 17
Should be
two quotation marks
in front of Casey Jones.

On page 18, line 26.
change *Rhinehart* to
Rineheart

On page 3, (1st sentence in the
book), put a comma after
trait and one after *few*.

On page 51, line 9.
Change *Litt.* to *Lit.*

On page 51, line 29,
Change *Cumizza* to *Cunizza*

On page 56, line 2
Change *Litt.* to *Lit.*

On page 80, line 29
Change *Cambell* to *Campbell*
or whatever correct spelling is.

Page 116, line 6.
Substitute *metier* for *flar*

Page 117, Line 30
Substitute Lit. for Litt.

Page 119, line 4
One dot is outside the
parenthesis

Page 180, line 24
Substitute *shimmee entheusiasticly.*
for *tickle-toe on the soft carpet*

Page 182, line 27
Substitute the word *utterly*
for the word *just*

P. 184, line 1
Should be *unimpeachable*
instead of *impeachable*

P 199, 4th line from bottom
Change *juvenalia* to juvenilia

Page 224, line 25
Change *M^ckenzie* to *Mackenzie*

Page 224, line 24
Change *Jenny* to *Jennie*

P. 228, line 23
Change *I restless* to
I am restless

P 229, line 17
Gunmeyer is not the correct
Spelling of this name.

Page 234, line 8
juvenilia instead of *juvenalia*

Page 235, line 14
delete comma after sight

P 235, line 23 should
read *was dead and sound not yet
awoken—Life cracked like ice!—
one brilliant ect*
(In other words, the word *life*
should be capitalized but not the
word *one*)

P 240
Are the genders right in fifth
line of poem?

P 251, Line 9
Stretch! should be *Scratch!*

P 296, line 27
deep should be *much*

Scribner's now had one list from Bridges and one from Fitzgerald. Perkins had the printers at the Scribner Press make the changes, and on 8 July he wrote Fitzgerald that the corrections had been made in the earliest possible printing—the fourth impression of May 1920. However, not all the changes that Fitzgerald asked for were made. No alteration was made in the French poem on page 240, and the error "juvenalia" for "juvenilia" was left on both pages mentioned by Fitzgerald.

So matters stood through May and June and two more printings of *This Side of Paradise*. By now the book was attracting notice and selling well. Word of its success spread to

England, and W. Collins Sons & Co., Ltd., of London agreed to bring out an edition for the British market. News of the up-coming typesetting reached Fitzgerald in Westport, Connecti-cut, where he and Zelda were living for the summer, and caused him to write to Perkins:

July 7th 1920

Dear Mr. Perkins:

   In regard to this English edition of *Paradise* I want to ask you a favor. It seems to me that if the book appears there in a land of much more intense scholarship with *approximately 100* mispellings and misprints it would hurt it.

   You already have at least two lists of corrections Mr Bridges + mine + I am putting down herewith an-other list of additional ones some Harvard scholar sent me. I have gotten several letters recently which indicate that it is rather a mistake to let the book go thru edition after edi-tion without corrections. Of course almost all the mistakes were mine but it was rather humiliating this morning to get a letter wondering whether "they left the mistakes in just as they did in the Young Visitors to keep the spirit of the original."

At the end of this letter, Fitzgerald put down his second list of corrections. Some of them had already been made in the plates; others were new.

Corrections (3d list)[2]

[page]	4	Change	Margaritta	to Margherita
"	7	"	Ashville	To Asheville

2. Fitzgerald was counting Bridges's list as number one, his own first list as number two, and this list, his second, as number three.

"	120	"	Dachari	to Daiquiori
"	154	"	Cecelia	to Cecilia
"	176	"	Johnston	to Johnson
"	229	"	Gunmyer	to Guynemer
"	232	"	Gouveneer	to Gouveneur
"	233	"	Bennet	to Bennett
"	240	"	langeur	to langueur
"	242	"	Celleni	to Cellini
"	252	"	tens	to teens
"	300	"	bon	to borne

If you can't find the other two lists I may be able to get another thorough list from some one.

F.S.F.

Fitzgerald was upset over the condition of his text. The letter mentioning *The Young Visiters* (Doran, 1919) must have rankled him especially. This novel, a faddish literary success, was supposedly written by a nine-year-old girl named Daisy Ashford. Her errors in spelling and word usage were preserved in the printed book, as the title shows. Fitzgerald could hardly have been pleased by the comparison, but it would shortly become a standard joke in American literary circles to refer to him as "the Princeton Daisy Ashford" because of the text of *This Side of Paradise*.[3]

The new errors in this second Fitzgerald list were changed (but not necessarily corrected) in the Scribner's plates, and the new readings appeared in the seventh impression of Au-

3. See, for example, Heywood Broun, "Paradise and Princeton," *New York Tribune*, 11 Apr. 1920, p. VII–9. Broun writes of Fitzgerald, "Daisy Ashford is hardly more naïve." Or see "Help! Help!" *Chicago Daily News*, 28 Apr. 1920, p. 12. This spoof letter refers to Fitzgerald as a "Princeton Daisy Ashford scribbling limericks on washroom walls and leaving off the last lines."

gust 1920. On 8 July, Perkins wrote to tell Fitzgerald what was being done about the English edition:

> As for the English edition, as they will set the book up, most of these corrections should be made by their proof-readers,—that is, unless proofreading in England has sunk to the level to which the war has somehow brought it here. We have virtually had to undertake to read typographically in the Editorial Department now, and that is a very different thing from the ordinary editorial reading which is done by way of making suggestions and criticism. It is purely the mechanical and therefore irksome. But to make sure that the English catch the mistakes, I will get together the lists you have sent and the one we have made and send a complete list to their editorial department.

Perkins had on hand one list from Bridges and two from Fitzgerald, and he seems to have conflated the three and sent that list to Collins in London. The conflated list is not in the Scribner Archive at Princeton, but judging from the English publisher's reply, one error was again not mentioned:

> 28th July 1920.
>
> Messrs Charles Scribner's Sons.,
>   Fifth Avenue at 48th Street,
>   NEW YORK.
> Gentlemen,
>   We are very much obliged to you for the corrections that you have sent us for "THIS SIDE OF PARADISE". We will read the book very carefully for press in any case and will see that these are incorporated. We notice one mistake

which you have not given in your list which is, that the author repeatedly uses the word juven*a*lia instead of juven*i*lia.[4]

On this side of the Atlantic, new criticism of *This Side of Paradise* was appearing. Franklin P. Adams in his *New York Tribune* column "The Conning Tower" for 6 July 1920 attacked Fitzgerald for writing a book that was "sloppy and cocky; impudent instead of confident; and verbose." Adams continued, "It is doubtful whether the Scribner proofreading is at fault for the numerous errors; and if they are the author's, they indicate a sloppy carelessness that it will pay Mr. Fitzgerald to overcome." Adams followed his remarks with a list of errors which he evidently got from a first, second, or third printing of *This Side of Paradise*, since some of them had by that time been changed in subsequent printings:

He speaks, for example, of "Frank on the Mississippi." The book is "Frank on the Lower Mississippi," as any slippered pantaloon who used to read Harry Castlemon will recall. Other instances of Mr. Fitzgerald's disregard for accuracy follow:

Ashville	[Compton] McKenzie
Collar and Daniel's	Fanny Hurst
"First-Year Latin"	Lorelie
Mary Roberts Rhinehart	"Ghunga Dhin"
cut a swathe	flambuoyant
[Swinburne's] "Poems and	"Come Into the Garden,
Ballades"	Maude"

---

4. Scribner Archive, quoted with the permission of Collins Publishers, London.

"Jenny Gerhardt"   flare [for *flair*]
                                    [Arnold] Bennet
                                    Gouveneer Morris[5]

Fitzgerald was troubled by these fresh evidences of error, and
he wrote Perkins again:

                                    Westport, Conn.
                                    July 16th, 1920
Dear Mr. Perkins:
    Last week in the Tribune F.P.A. balled out my book and
gave a long list of mispellings—I find by looking at the
sixth edition that many of those first list of corrections
havn't been made—for instance *juvenalia* (twice) in the
section called "Tom the Censor" in "Experiments in Convalescense." I really think it has been a mistake to let it go
so long.
    . . . .

                                    Sincerely
                                    F Scott Fitz

    F.P.A. finds the following new misspellings
Frank on the Mississippi should be *Frank on the Lower
Mississippi*

                                                    Chap I
Collar + Daniel's First-Year Latin   (mispelt)
                                                 Chap I
Cut a swathe (mispelt) Chap II
Poems + Ballades should be *Poems + Ballads*
                                        (Chap II)
Fanny Hurst should be Fannie Hurst
Lorelie (mispelt)
Ghunga Dhin (mispelt)

5. The bracketed information was supplied by Adams and appears here as
it did in his column.

Flambuoyant (mispelt
Come Into the Garden, Maude. (mispelt?)

F.P.A. was not through with *This Side of Paradise*. In his 14 July column he published a second collection of errors that had been given to him by someone with the initials "C.W."

inexplicably (for inextricably)	Christie Mathewson
Mont Martre	confectionary
tetotalling	Lyoff Tolstoi
Samuel Johnston	Juvenalia
Celleni	forborne
stimulous	born (for borne)

Fitzgerald, still anxious to fix up his novel, sent a postcard to Perkins three days later giving his fourth and last list of errors:

Westport, Conn.
July 17th 1920

F.P.A. is at it again. Here is his latest list

Old	*New Ones*
juvenalia	Christie Mathewson
born for borne	confectionary
Cellini	Lyoff Tolstoi
Samuel Johnston	forborne
	inexplicably for
	inextricably
	Mont Martre
	tetotalling
	stimulous

Havn't my copy of the book so don't know where these occur

Sincerely
F Scott Fitzgerald

With Fitzgerald's third and fourth lists in hand, Perkins did some checking and wrote back on 30 July. He too was disappointed about the doggedly erroneous condition of *This Side of Paradise* and said he would try to correct these latest mistakes. Perkins promised to send Fitzgerald a list of changes already made, and to send the Scribner Press another list of changes that still needed to be made.

For his last two lists, Fitzgerald had not given Perkins page or line references to the readings, and so only one of the new errors was located: Kipling's "Ghunga Dhin" at 18.22 was changed (but not corrected) to "Gunga Dhin." Also the *correct* reading "Rinehart" at 18.26 (which itself was a plate change over erroneous "Rhinehart" of the first three printings) was altered again to read "Rineheart," the wrong spelling Fitzgerald had suggested in his first list. These two changes, like the ones from Fitzgerald's third list, appeared in the seventh printing. That ended the work on the plates of *This Side of Paradise*.

Here one should pause and count up the number of lists that were made: (1) Robert Bridges's list of 1 April; (2) Fitzgerald's first list, compiled in early April; (3) the list sent to Fitzgerald by the Harvard man; (4) Fitzgerald's second list, made for the English edition and included in a 7 July letter to Perkins; (5) Perkins's conflated list which he sent to London in early July; (6) F.P.A.'s first list in his column for 6 July; (7) Fitzgerald's third list, occasioned by F.P.A.'s first list—this list was sent to Perkins on 16 July; (8) the list put together by "C.W." and published in F.P.A.'s column for 14 July; (9) Fitzgerald's fourth list, copied from "C.W.'s" list—this list was sent to Perkins on 17 July; (10) Perkins's list of changes that had already been made, which he told Fitzgerald he was going to send to him; (11) Perkins's list of errors that still needed to be corrected, which he told Fitzgerald that he would send to the Scribner Press for the next printing.

With so much effort going into the making of lists, one wonders what happened to the plates. The machine collation on pp. 112–13 tells the story. There are no unexplained changes; each plate variant is mentioned in at least one of the lists above. But this table shows only changes. Some errors were corrected in one spot but left standing in another. For example, "Bennet" at 233.14 was altered to "Bennett," but a second "Bennet" referring to the same English novelist was left at 224.25. "Ashville" at 7.33 was changed to "Asheville," but another "Ashville" five lines above on the same page was untouched. Other errors mentioned by Fitzgerald were not corrected: for instance, "flambuoyant" at 49.15, "Juvenalia" at 234.8 and 235.2, and "juvenalia" at 199.29 were all left alone. There are also errors in the text of the first edition that were not noticed by any of the list-makers. See, for example, "PARASIDE" in the running title on p. 50, "a tri-cornered conversation between" at 109.24, "Lafayette Esquadrille" at 112.23 and 119.14, "the latter of these three" at 131.21, and "several time a week" at 139.21.

A record of Fitzgerald's attempts to mend the text of *This Side of Paradise* survives in his personal marked copy of the novel, which has numerous corrections penciled on its pages. Fitzgerald also made several stylistic revisions in the text of his copy. Some of these changes were sent to Perkins and were made in the plates; other changes were never called to Perkins's attention and have never appeared in any text of *This Side of Paradise*.[6]

Fitzgerald's novel did well in America: some 49,000 copies were sold between March 1920 and October 1921—an excellent record for a first book. Evidence suggests, however, that sales would have been higher had Scribner's used aggressive marketing techniques like those being employed by such

6. Matthew J. Bruccoli, "Fitzgerald's Marked Copy of *This Side of Paradise*," *Fitzgerald/Hemingway Annual 1971*, pp. 64–69.

Plate Changes in the First Edition of *This Side of Paradise*

Page & Line	First Printing	Fourth Printing	Seventh Printing
[v]	SIGORNEY	SIGOURNEY	
3.1	trait	trait,	
3.2	few	few,	
4.1	Margaritta		Margherita
6.7	raconteur	raconteuse	
7.33	Ashville		Asheville
17.3	'Casey-Jones	"Casey-Jones	
18.22	"Ghunga Dhin,"		"Gunga Dhin,"
18.26	Rhinehart	Rinehart	Rineheart
28.10	ex-ambassador	ex-minister	
51.9	Litt.	Lit.	
51.29	*Cumizza*	*Cunizza*	
56.2	*Litt.*	*Lit.*	
80.29	Cambell	Campbell	
116.6	flare	metier	
117.30	*Litt.*	*Lit.*	
119.4	*Booth . . .).*	*Booth . . .)*	
120.13	Dachari	Daiquiri	
154.—	CECELIA		CECILIA
176.36	JOHNSTON		JOHNSON
180.24	*tickle-toe on the soft carpet*	*shimmy enthusiastically*	

"modern" firms as Boni & Liveright or Doubleday. Instead of ordering two or three large print runs and attempting to fill the bookstores with copies of *This Side of Paradise*, Scribner's played it safe and printed twelve successive small impressions of from 2,000 to 5,000 copies. These figures suggest that the publisher waited until orders came in before printing books to fill them. Scribner's apparently suspected that the success of *This Side of Paradise* was freakish and temporary, and the firm was anxious not to be caught with back stock on its hands. After thirteenth and fourteenth printings of 1,000 and

Page & Line	First Printing	Fourth Printing	Seventh Printing
182.27	*just*	*utterly*	
184.1	*impeachable*	*unimpeachable*	
224.24	Jenny	Jennie	
224.25	McKenzie	Mackenzie	
226.35	Benêt	Benét	
228.23	I restless	I am restless	
229.13	Kerenski	Kerensky	
229.17	Gunmeyer	Guynemer	
232.22	Gouveneer	Gouverneur	
233.14	Bennet		Bennett
235.14	*sight,*	*sight*	
235.23	*life*	*Life*	
235.24	*One*	*—one*	
240.28	*langeur*		*langueur*
242.26	Celleni		Cellini
251.9	Stretch!	Scratch!	
252.34	tens		teens
294.23	Mackeys	Mackays	
296.27	deep	much	
300.27	born		borne
304.19	God's	Gods	

970 copies in 1922, Scribner's leased the plates to A. L. Burt, a reprint house, for a "cheap edition." After that, Scribner's ordered small impressions of 270 copies in 1925 and 290 in 1931—these to keep *This Side of Paradise* technically in print.

Scribner's should not be faulted for this sales approach. Their strategy was standard for a conservative publisher. They had never handled a book like *This Side of Paradise* and did not wish to overcommit their resources. Scribner's did not make the same mistake with Fitzgerald's next novel, *The Beautiful and Damned* (1922). Over forty thousand copies were ready for shipping on publication day; booksellers did not have to wait to get Fitzgerald's second novel on their bookshelves.[7]

The circulation of *This Side of Paradise* would undoubtedly have been helped by a paperback edition in 1921 or 1922, but in the twenties there were no paperback publishers as we know them today. Most students of the period assume that the technology for manufacturing paperbacks had not yet been developed, but that is not true. American printers had been able to produce paperbacks at least since the 1830s, but the entry of paperbound books on the market in mass quantities, once in the early 1840s and again in the 1870s and 1880s, had in each instance wrecked the price structure of the publishing industry. The second period of mass paperback publication, from about 1870 to 1893, had been particularly ruinous and had only been halted by passage in Congress of an international copyright law in 1891 and by a major business panic two years later.

In 1920 American trade publishers were extremely leery of another bout with paperbacks. The senior executives and editors of Scribner's could remember the price wars of the 1880s very well, and Scribner's itself had recently lost a lengthy and expensive court action against Macy's department store over the issue of price-cutting and "loss-leadering." No responsible publisher wanted anything to do with inexpensive books; publishers preferred not even to handle the "cheap editions" of their own novels. This situation worked against Fitzgerald, for if ever a book would have sold well to young readers in paperback, that book was *This Side of Paradise*. A paperbound edition would have provided Fitzgerald with some income

7. These figures are taken from Matthew J. Bruccoli, *F. Scott Fitzgerald: A Descriptive Bibliography* (Pittsburgh: University of Pittsburgh Press, 1972), pp. 15–20, 40.

from year to year and would have kept his name in the book-shops between novels. But the American publishing trade was not structured that way in the twenties, and as a result *This Side of Paradise* went quickly from hardback bestseller to A. L. Burt reprint to backlist title, where it was largely forgotten by the reading public.

Across the Atlantic, the history of the novel took a curious twist with the publication of the first English edition by Collins in May 1921. It differs from the first American edition in some 850 readings. A few of these variants were justifiable improvements: 42 seem to derive from the conflated list that Perkins sent to Collins, while others are independent corrections of obvious errors. But most of the remaining hundreds of variants were designed to Anglicize the novel, to make typically American features of punctuation and spelling conform to British usage. Words like "favored" and "realized" became "favoured" and "realised"; an automobile had a "tyre," not a "tire"; people wrote "cheques," not "checks," and said "Hallo" instead of "Hello." Stylistically the effect was to make Amory Blaine something of a Yank at Oxford. That effect was subtly reinforced by Collins's imposition of contemporary British punctuation on *This Side of Paradise*. Double quotation marks became single and vice versa, and abbreviations did not end with periods.

Two other significant editions of *This Side of Paradise* have been published, both under the Scribner imprint, the first in 1960 and the second in 1970. A hand collation of the 1920 first edition against the 1960 typesetting reveals no fresh authority. In fact the 1960 edition is much worse than the 1920 text. There are 190 variants, a figure that does not include minor features of typography or word division. Of the 190 differences, 40 enter the 1960 text legitimately from plate changes in the first edition. Twenty of the remaining 150 changes are substantive, but only one of those is a justified correction. The other 19 variants are corruptions. Words are added, dropped, and changed; the reading "fact" becomes "face," "*head*" becomes "*hear*," and "a great lot" becomes "a great deal," for instance. Errors from the 1920 text are reset without correction, and many new mistakes in spelling and punctuation are introduced. Sometime in the early 1970s Scribner's tried to patch up this text. Nine errors were corrected in the plates, but a great many mistakes were not noticed. These include "threatre" at 59.11, "savior faire" at 76.17, "successs" at 98.4, "tabacco" at 255.11, and "stimulous" at 273.28. Also uncorrected are "*Juvenalia*" at 218.25, "Juvenalia" at 219.17, and "juvenalia" at 186.20.

The 1970 Scribner's edition is a better text than its 1960 predecessor. The two derive independently from the 1920 setting, and so the 1970 text does not inherit corruptions from the 1960 edition. The 1970 text was prepared with some attention to accuracy: "Asheville," "Gunga Din," "Mary Roberts Rinehart," and "stimulus" are spelled correctly, and only a few corruptions in punctuation are introduced. Numerous errors still survive in its text, however. These include "confectionary" at 41.25, "Lafayette Esquadrille" at 98.33 and 104.27, "the latter of these three" at 114.16, and "Fanny Hurst" at 197.37. Perhaps inevitably, the 1970 text prints "juvenalia" at 172.7 and "Juvenalia" at 199.11 and 199.37. Although better than the 1960 setting, the 1970 Scribner's edition is still not a particularly good text. It has never been available on the commercial market; it was sold only during the early 1970s through book-of-the-month and cookbook clubs as one volume of a four-volume set of Fitzgerald's novels, offered as a bonus to new subscribers. The text of *This Side of Paradise* currently on the market is the patched-up 1960 setting. It is distributed as a Scribner Library paperback and is widely used by students, teachers, and even by publishing scholars.

This Side of Paradise has been subjected to heavy criticism since its original publication. Edmund Wilson, in his first essay on Fitzgerald, wrote that the novel "is one of the most illiterate books of any merit ever published (a fault which the publisher's wretched proof-reading apparently made no effort to correct). It is not only full of bogus ideas and faked literary references but it is full of English words misused with the most reckless abandon."[8] Fitzgerald was embarrassed by the text of *This Side of Paradise*. In the novel he had flaunted his familiarity with books, poems, critics, authors, and philosophers. He had attempted to balance his showiness with a good dose of irony, but the misspelled words, incorrect titles, and wrong names undercut his attitude and mocked him. Errors in spelling, grammar, and usage—whether authorial or not— never add to the "charm" of a novel. Instead they invite condescension. Shortly after publication of the book, while F.P.A. was printing lists of errors in the *Tribune*, Philip C. Gunion published this paragraph in *Printer's Ink*:

> Franklin P. Adams, from his Conning Tower in the New York *Tribune*, looks down on Mr. Fitzgerald and sees some glaring mistakes in spelling and allusions, and feels disappointed because the young author is not a finished writer. Read the book and agree with me that if he had stopped to remove the crudities from his style he never could have painted such vivid word pictures of contemporary life of a certain class and of a certain age. In addition the sense is there, for we know who "Mary Roberts Rineheart" is even if Fitzgerald does misspell her last name and when

8. "The Literary Spotlight," *Bookman* 55 (Mar. 1922): 22.

he says, "Amory stood under the glass portcullis of a theatre" we know he meant porte-cochere and feel a glow of warmth at our superior knowledge.[9]

The errors in *This Side of Paradise* invite this attitude. If one really wants Fitzgerald's errrors, then one needs a facsimile edition of the manuscript. A facsimile would show all of Fitzgerald's mistakes, not just those that slipped by editors and proofreaders, and it would not contain the many nonauthorial errors and corruptions which have crept into published editions. On the other hand, if one wants to judge *This Side of Paradise* as a finished work of literature, one must have a properly edited text.

Fitzgerald remained aware of the errors in *This Side of Paradise* for the rest of his life. He once inscribed a copy of the novel: "This book is a history of mistakes—something never retracted yet, in a way, to be ashamed of, by a conscientious worker."[10] In 1938 he proposed a kind of retraction by trying to persuade Scribner's to reissue the novel. He had given up hope of getting the errors corrected and was toying instead with the idea of composing a "glossary of absurdities and inaccuracies" for the printing.[11] This scheme to turn errors into assets never materialized, however. No new impression was issued, and no such glossary survives. Two years later, by now virtually unknown and unread, Fitzgerald tried to resurrect his early books. On 13 December 1940 he wrote Perkins to ask how much it would cost to buy the plates of *This Side of Paradise*, presumably so that another publisher or he himself could

9. "A Novelist Disciple of Old Man Specific," *Printer's Ink*, 28 Oct. 1920, p. 100.

10. Reprinted from a 1961 House of Books catalogue in *Fitzgerald Newsletter* (Washington, D.C.: Microcard, 1969), p. 80. The inscription is undated.

11. *Dear Scott/Dear Max*, p. 251.

reissue it.[12] But that idea too was stillborn. Fitzgerald died eight days later, on 21 December 1940. Most of the people who knew his name remembered him as the chronicler of the flapper and the flivver, as a man who had outlived his time—as the author of *This Side of Paradise*.

The faulty text of the novel is the only one that has ever been available to Fitzgerald readers and scholars. Surely the time has now come for an edition of *This Side of Paradise* as Fitzgerald would have originally wanted it done. The errors in the book are significant—they figure in its initial reception and subsequent reputation—but many of these mistakes are not Fitzgerald's. Blame for the sloppy text must be distributed all along the line of textual transmission. Fitzgerald deserves much of this blame, but as he wrote years later, "My God—did they expect me to spell? If I was such a hot shot couldn't the proof-readers do the spelling?"[13]

The errors in *This Side of Paradise* should not be perpetuated. We are not getting the flavor of Fitzgerald's idiosyncratic orthography and word usage; we are only getting a book marred by careless error. A properly edited text would make all previous editions what they deserve to be: literary artifacts of historical importance only.

12. *Dear Scott/Dear Max*, p. 268.
13. "Early Success," p. 97.

Appendixes

A. Physical Characteristics of the *Romantic Egotist* Fragments

CHAPTER I—"The Egotist Up"

Black double-spaced carbon typescript; white wove unlined and unwatermarked paper; square corners and no notebook holes; 215 × 279 mm.; pagination [1], 2–4, [5], 6–34 in typed numerals; black-ink revisions in Fitzgerald's hand on page [5] only.

CHAPTER II—"The Egotist Down"

Black double-spaced ribbon typescript; white wove unlined paper; watermarked "[crest device] | YORKSHIRE BOND"; round corners and three notebook holes; 216 × 279 mm.; pagination 1–19 in penciled holograph numerals—unknown hand; black-ink and penciled revisions in Fitzgerald's hand throughout.

CHAPTER V—"Spires and Gargoiles"

Black double-spaced carbon typescript; white wove unlined and unwatermarked paper; square corners and no notebook holes; 214 × 277 mm.; two systems of pagination, penciled in unknown hands—System I is 20–43, System II is [1], 2–3, [4], 5, [6–7], 8, [9–11], 12, [13], 14, [15–16], 17–24; two penciled revisions in Fitzgerald's hand on p. 39.

CHAPTER XII—"Eleanor"

Purple double-spaced carbon typescript; pp. 1–17 are white wove unlined paper; watermarked "HAMMERMILL | BOND"; pp. 18–21 are white wove unlined paper; watermarked "CRAFTSMAN BOND | [device]"; square corners and no notebook holes; 214 × 278 mm.; pagination 1–21, penciled in an unknown hand; black-ink revisions in Fitzgerald's hand throughout.

CHAPTER XIV—"The Devil"

Black double-spaced carbon typescript; white wove unlined paper; watermarked only on pp. 4–10, but all paper is of identical stock; watermarked "524 BOND"; square corners and no notebook holes; 215 × 278 mm.; two systems of pagination, penciled in unknown hands—System I is [1–3], 4–11, [12]; System II is 22–24, [unnumbered page], 25–32; black-ink revisions by Fitzgerald throughout; revisions are infrequent and minor.

B. Physical Characteristics
of the Manuscript

1. Pagination

Pagination: 1–2, [3–11 missing], 12–19, 20+21+22 (a single leaf), 23–74, 74½, 75–104, 104½, 105–27, 127½, 128–60, 160½, 161–68, 168½, 169–263, 263½, 264–88, 288½, 289–339, 339½, 340–94, 394A–394F, 395–408, 408A–408C, 409–15, 415A, [415B unnumbered], 416–89, 489A–489C, 490–505, 506+507 (a single leaf), 508–64, 566–626. The missing pp. 3–11 would have been the holograph draft of Fitzgerald's preface, which was not published with the novel. Someone, presumably Fitzgerald, substituted a later TS of the preface at this point in the MS.

2. *Romantic Egotist/This Side of Paradise*
Typescript Sheets

Pagination: 197, 198, 201, 206, 207, 216, 217, 218, 219, 224, 230, 231, 235, 241, 244, 245, 246, 258, 260, 277, 278, 279, 289, 290, 291, 295, 296, 302, 303, 306, 307, 308, 311, 312, 313, 314, 325, 326, 327, 328, 329, 330, 337, 341, 346, 350, 352, 353, 356, 361, 362, 363, 364, 365. These sheets are black double-spaced ribbon typescript on white wove unlined paper watermarked "[device] | YORKSHIRE BOND"; the corners are rounded and there are three notebook holes along the left side of each sheet; the sheets measure 216 × 279 mm.

3. Other Typescript Sheets

Leaf 367 is a black double-spaced carbon typescript of un-determined origin, typed on white wove unlined unwater-marked stock measuring 214 × 278 mm.

Leaf 378 (Father Fay's poem) is a black single-spaced rib-bon typescript on white wove unlined unwatermarked stock measuring 215 × 279 mm.

Leaves 389–90, 394, 395–408 (from the *Smart Set* type-script of "The Débutante") are black single-spaced carbon typescripts; leaves 389–90, 394, and 395–402 are white wove unlined stock watermarked "HAMMERMILL | BOND" and measuring 213 × 278 mm.; leaves 403–8 are white wove unwatermarked stock measuring 212 × 275 mm. (Although typewritten on two different papers, these "Débutante" sheets are parts of the same carbon typescript; the typist shifted to a new paper midway through the carbon copy.)

Leaves 498–501, 506+507 (a single leaf), 515, 516, and 517 (from the short-story typescript of "Young Irony") are black single-spaced ribbon typescripts on white wove unlined stock watermarked "HAMMERMILL | BOND" and measur-ing 214 × 278 mm.

Leaf 521 is a black single-spaced carbon typescript of un-determined origin, typed on white wove unwatermarked stock measuring 215 × 277 mm.

Leaf 522 is a black single-spaced ribbon typescript of un-determined origin, typed on white wove unlined unwater-marked stock measuring 214 × 279 mm.

4. Holograph Sheets

Through page 243 of the manuscript, the holograph passages are inscribed on white wove paper which is sometimes unwatermarked and sometimes watermarked "HAMMERMILL | BOND." The watermark usually appears on every fourth sheet. These holograph sheets measure 215 × 279 mm. After page 243, all holograph inscription is on a coarse, wove unwatermarked off-white stock measuring 217 × 281 mm. Pages 1–2, 71, 74½, 104½, 127½, 160½, and 168½ are also inscribed on this same coarse wove paper, indicating that these sheets were added to the manuscript after the inscription of page 243.

C. Manuscript–First Edition
Conversion Table

The table that follows makes it possible to trace, in the text of the Scribner's 1920 first edition, those passages that originated in the manuscript as holograph drafts, or as revised typescript sheets from *The Romantic Egotist*, or as revised typescript sheets from other sources. Comparison of these passages with respect to style, tone, and point-of-view helps explain the several narrative stances and prose textures in the published novel.

In the table below, the manuscript page numbers in the left-hand column stand for inclusive blocks of MS material that are homogeneous. These numbers are followed in the second column by a description of the character of those pages, whether holograph, holograph insert, or some variety of typescript. The third column records page-line references to passages in the first edition which correspond to the text inscribed or typed on the MS page(s). The fourth column gives the first and last words of the passage inscribed or typed on the MS page(s). A sample entry is as follows:

23–74 (Holograph) 5.11–23.33 "I . . . bourgeoisie.

This entry indicates that pages 23–74 inclusive in the MS are holograph. This text is printed in the first edition from line 11 of page 5 to line 33 of page 23. The first reading inscribed on MS p. 23 is "*I*, which is printed in the first edition at 5.11. The final reading inscribed on MS p. 74 is *bourgeoisie.*, which is printed in the first edition at 23.33. The only unusual abbreviation is "RE/TSOP TS" which indicates a sheet or sheets from typescript of *The Romantic Egotist* that Fitzgerald spliced into the manuscript of *This Side of Paradise*.

MS Page(s)		First Edition Passages	
1–19	(Holograph)	[iii].1–4.33	THIS . . . read
20+21+22	(Holograph)	4.33–5.10	to . . . right."
23–74	(Holograph)	5.11–23.33	"I . . . bourgeoisie.
74½	(Holograph insert)	23.33–24.12	I . . . school."
75–104	(Holograph)	24.13–35.10	"Yes . . . before.
104½	(Holograph insert)	35.10–24	He . . . as a
105–27	(Holograph)	35.24–45.28	matter . . . song, a song
127½	(Holograph insert)	45.28–46.1	with . . . down
128–60	(Holograph)	46.1–58.2	the . . . mirror.
160½	(Holograph insert)	58.3–14	One . . . trying
161–68	(Holograph)	58.14–60.34	to . . . sprang
168½	(Holograph insert)	60.34–61.11	to . . . reaction.
169–96	(Holograph)	61.——70.19	"HA-HA . . . while
197–98	(RE/TSOP TS)	70.19–72.24	the shifting . . . grape-shot.
199–200	(Holograph)	72.25–73.11	"I've . . . were
201	(RE/TSOP TS)	73.11–74.18	distinctly . . . down-stairs.
202–5	(Holograph)	74.19–75.35	Boys . . . whether
206–7	(RE/TSOP TS)	75.35–78.10	or . . . lost

MS Page(s)		First Edition Passages	
208–15	(Holograph)	78.10–81.11	his . . . since
216–19	(RE/TSOP TS)	81.11–85.19	he . . . she
220–23	(Holograph)	85.19–87.6	giggled . . . found
224	(RE/TSOP TS)	87.6–88.17	them . . . not
225–29	(Holograph)	88.17–90.1	deliberately . . . really?"
230–31	(RE/TSOP TS)	90.2–91.31	"Yes . . . Monday."
232–34	(Holograph)	91.32–92.24	They . . . just going to
235	(RE/TSOP TS)	92.24–93.24	disorganize . . . sensualist
236–40	(Holograph)	93.24–95.8	really . . . and
241	(RE/TSOP TS)	95.8–96.12	then . . . sound.
242–43	(Holograph)	96.— –96.33	CRESCENDO . . . before.
244–46	(RE/TSOP TS)	97.1–100.7	The . . . meaning.
247–57	(Holograph)	100.8–104.26	"Isabelle . . . say."
258	(RE/TSOP TS)	104.27–105.31/2	"Why . . . anagrams.
259	(Holograph)	105.32–106.9	He . . . room.
260	(RE/TSOP TS)	106.10–107.8	"If . . . over."
261–63	(Holograph)	107.9–108.23	He . . . Maybe."
263½	(Holograph insert)	108.24–109.7	Amory's . . . Amory.
264–76	(Holograph)	109.— –112.24	FINANCIAL . . . Esquadrille."
277–78	(RE/TSOP TS)	112.25–114.23	"You . . . collecting
279	(RE/TSOP TS and Holograph)	114.23–115.13	collecting . . . your
280–88	(Holograph)	115.13–117.25	springs . . . He
288½	(Holograph insert)	117.25–30	was . . . *Litt.*
289	(RE/TSOP TS)	117.31–119.6	"Good . . . affirmative
290	(RE/TSOP TS and Holograph)	119.7–18	The . . . afterward.

MS Page(s)		First Edition Passages	
291	(RE/TSOP TS)	119.— –120.21	THE . . . harmless,
292–94	(Holograph)	120.21–121.25	ended . . . fizz— and
295–96	(RE/TSOP TS)	121.25–123.30	everything's . . . goodness.
297–301	(Holograph)	123.31–125.29	"Well . . . put his
302–3	(RE/TSOP TS)	125.29–127.30	face . . . again?"
304–5	(Holograph)	127.31–128.25	Simultaneously . . . lay
306–7	(RE/TSOP TS)	128.25–130.18	for . . . out
308	(RE/TSOP TS and Holograph)	130.18–131.10	of . . . before
309–10	(Holograph)	131.10–132.5	him . . . bout.
311–14	(RE/TSOP TS)	132.6–136.11	"No . . . processes
315–24	(Holograph)	136.11–139.30	of . . . man's
325–29	(RE/TSOP TS)	139.30–144.21	make-up . . . odd."
330	(RE/TSOP TS and Holograph)	144.22–145.17	"He's . . . walk
331–36	(Holograph)	145.17–148.1	after . . . length
337	(RE/TSOP TS)	148.1–149.5	of . . . innocently.
338–39	(Holograph)	149.6–31	"What . . . Club.
339½	(Holograph insert)	149.32–150.7	As . . . that
340	(Holograph)	150.7–18	your . . . Sorrow
341	(RE/TSOP TS)	150.18–151.14	lay . . . she
342–45	(Holograph)	151.14–152.29	could . . . "Tell
346	(RE/TSOP TS)	152.29–153.30	me . . . She
347–49	(Holograph)	153.30–155.1	did . . . Clara
350	(RE/TSOP TS)	155.1–35	hesitated . . . on."
351	(Holograph)	156.1–16	"I . . . chance."
352–53	(RE/TSOP TS)	156.17–158.17	"Well . . . to
354–55	(Holograph)	158.17–159.14	marry . . . she
356	(RE/TSOP TS)	159.14–160.15	announced . . . gold . . ."
357–60	(Holograph)	160.— –161.31	AMORY . . . idealists

MS Page(s)		First Edition Passages	
361–65	(RE/TSOP TS)	161.31–167.4	you meet . . . magnificence."
366	(Holograph)	167.5–15	"God . . . trees.
367	(Untraced TS)	167.16–168.10	"You . . . *land,*
368–77	(Holograph)	168.10–173.1	*the sunny* . . . is:
378	(Fay's TS poem)	173.2–174.5	*A Lament* . . . Ochone."
379–88	(Holograph)	174.6–[177].2	Amory— Amory . . . PERSONAGE
389–90	(*Smart Set* "Débutante" TS)	179.— –181.8	CHAPTER . . . *room.)*
391–93	(Holograph)	181.9–182.13	CECELIA . . . family.
394	(*Smart Set* "Débutante" TS)	182.14–27	CECELIA . . . enters.
394A–394F	(Holograph insert)	182.27–185.2	ROSALIND . . . one.
395–408	(*Smart Set* "Débutante" TS)	185.3–199.7	CECELIA . . . *again.)*
408A–408C	(Holograph insert)	199.— –200.3	KISMET . . . streets . . .
409–15	(Holograph)	200.3–202.23	it . . . hours.
415A–[415B]	(Holograph insert)	202.— –203.18	AQUATIC . . . optimists.
416–89	(Holograph)	203.— –235.2	FIVE . . . editions."
489A–489C	(Holograph insert)	235.— –236.3	LOOKING . . . BOY:—
490–97	(Holograph)	236.4–239.20	Your . . . for:
498–501	("Young Irony" short-story TS)	239.21–247.4	. . . But . . . darkness.
502–5	(Holograph)	247.— –248.21	SEPTEMBER . . . they
506+507	("Young Irony" short-story TS)	248.21–249.30	revelled . . . later.
508–14	(Holograph)	249.31–251.26	Often . . . golden
515–17	("Young Irony" short-story TS)	251.26–257.16	token . . . open.

MS Page(s)		First Edition Passages	
518–20	(Holograph)	257.17–258.31	"Eleanor . . . June.
521	(Untraced poem TS)	258.32–259.—	Here . . . STORM"
522	(Untraced poem TS)	259.17–260.17	"Faint . . . laughter . . ."
523–626	(Holograph)	261.— –305.6	CHAPTER . . . all."

D. Variants Between the First English and American Editions

The following table records major variants between the first English edition and the first American edition. All substantive variants are reported, together with a selection of representative accidentals. Variants marked with an asterisk result from the list sent to Collins by Maxwell Perkins, for they match alterations in the American plates ordered by him.

English		American	
[v]*	SIGOURNEY	[v]	SIGORNEY
3.1*	trait,	3.1	~ ʌ
3.2*	few,	3.2	~ ʌ
3.29*	Margherita	4.1	Margaritta
4.33	*Do and Dare,*	4.33	"Do and Dare,"
5.23	gibly	5.26	glibly
6.1*	raconteuse	6.7	raconteur
7.20*	Asheville	7.28	Ashville
7.25*	Asheville	7.33	Ashville
9.36	favoured	10.13	favored
10.6	realised	10.19	realized
13.13	too——	13.34	~—
17.21–22*	*Ghanga	Dhin;*	18.22	"Ghunga Dhin,"
17.25*	Rinehart	18.26	Rhinehart
19.22	unscrupulous	20.24	unscrupulousness
26.28*	ex-Minister	28.10	ex-ambassador
26.29	Ages,	28.11	~ ʌ

English		American	
29.26	a-hemmed	31.14	hemmed
39.6	suit-case	41.6	suitcase
39.28	confectionery	41.28	confectionary
43.33	back:—	46.4	~:
47.13	teetotalling	49.24	tetotalling
48.31*	Lit.	51.9	Litt.
48.37	Hallo	51.15	Hello
49.13*	*Cunizza*	51.29	*Cumizza*
51.26	all over the school	54.11	all over school
52.24–25	*Come | into the Garden, Maud,*	55.11–12	"Come into | the Garden, Maude,"
53.11*	*Lit.*	56.2	*Litt.*
61.34	arrangements	65.5	engagements
63.29	lashes	67.3	eyelashes
69.—	Wood	73.—	Woods
73.26	cosy	77.19	cosey
74.15	At a quarter	78.8	At quarter
76.34*	Campbell	80.29	Cambell
78.17	*night that loses*	82.17	*light that loses*
81.3	curtseys	85.10	courtesies
91.4	8.10	95.22	8:10
99.3	dresssing	103.16	dressing
101.9	cry,—	105.24	cry:
104.5	the	108.27	his
105.16	cheques	110.4	checks
111.23*	*métier*	116.6	flare
113.8*	*Lit.*	117.30	*Litt.*
114.19*	*Booth . . .)*	119.4	*Booth . . .).*
115.27*	Daiquiri	120.13	Dachari
123.37	his	129.5	this
124.35	round	130.5	around
129.27	Tolstoy	134.35	Tolstoi
131.14	more real	136.28	realler
133.15	feeling	138.32	feelings
134.2	times	139.21	time
135.16	blonde	140.35	blond
148.—*	Cecilia	154.—	Cecelia
156.12	good-bye	163.3	good-by
156.16	fanatic	163.6	~,

English		American	
167.21	is white	173.11	is as white
169.38	sizeable	175.26	sizable
170.19	bourgeois	176.3	burgeois
171.12*	'SAMUEL JOHNSON.'	176.36	SAMUEL JOHNSTON.
176.22*	*shimmy enthusiastically*	180.24	*tickle-toe on the soft carpet*
178.21*	*utterly*	182.27	*just*
179.28*	*unimpeachable*	184.1	*impeachable*
187.2	it.	191.32	~ ˄
190.14–15	you're │ — remarkable	195.15–16	you're re- │ markable
192.16	tyre	197.23	tire
194.21	juvenilia	199.29	juvenalia
197.5	he never	202.22	he had never
197.28	dive	203.12	dove
208.2	physical	214.5	physcal
217.31*	*Jennie*	224.24	Jenny
217.31*	Mackenzie	224.25	McKenzie
217.32	Bennett	224.25	Bennet
219.36*	Benét	226.35	Benêt
221.22*	I am restless	228.23	I restless
222.8	Lenin	229.12	Lenine
222.9*	Kerensky	229.13	Kerenski
222.13*	Guynemer	229.17	Gunmeyer
225.10*	Gouverneur	232.21	Gouveneer
225.34*	Bennett	233.14	Bennet
226.29	Juvenilia	234.8	Juvenalia
227.20	Juvenilia	235.2	Juvenalia
227.32*	*sight*	235.14	*sight,*
228.7*	*Life*	235.23	*life*
228.8*	*—one*	235.24	One
230.1	afterwards	238.1	afterward
232.29*	*langueur*	240.28	*langeur*
234.25*	Cellini	242.26	Celleni
242.23*	Scratch!	251.9	Stretch!
244.7*	teens	252.34	tens
244.12	Through	253.4	Thru
254.6	the eddy	263.9	an eddy
263.4	*graying*	273.4	*greying*

English		American	
276.27–28	had- | harmonised	287.18–19	had | harmonized
278.34	run I'd	289.31	I'd run
280.12	trade unions	291.15	trades-unions
283.12*	Mackays	294.23	Mackeys
283.19	stimulus	294.30	stimulous
285.12*	much profundity	296.27	deep profundity
289.2*	borne	300.27	born
289.27–28*	made. | him	301.18–19	made | him
292.12	reverie	304.15	revery
292.16*	Gods	304.19	God's

Index

www.ingramcontent.com/pod-product-compliance
Lightning Source LLC
Chambersburg PA
CBHW020332100426
42812CB00029B/3102/J